Communications
in Computer and Information Science 696

Commenced Publication in 2007
Founding and Former Series Editors:
Alfredo Cuzzocrea, Dominik Ślęzak, and Xiaokang Yang

More information about this series at http://www.springer.com/series/7899

Florian Daniel · Martin Gaedke (Eds.)

Rapid Mashup Development Tools

Second International Rapid Mashup Challenge, RMC 2016
Lugano, Switzerland, June 6, 2016
Revised Selected Papers

 Springer

Editors
Florian Daniel
Politecnico di Milano
Milano
Italy

Martin Gaedke
TU Chemnitz
Chemnitz
Germany

ISSN 1865-0929   ISSN 1865-0937   (electronic)
Communications in Computer and Information Science
ISBN 978-3-319-53173-1   ISBN 978-3-319-53174-8   (eBook)
DOI 10.1007/978-3-319-53174-8

Library of Congress Control Number: 2017930644

Printed on acid-free paper

This Springer imprint is published by Springer Nature
The registered company is Springer International Publishing AG
The registered company address is: Gewerbestrasse 11, 6330 Cham, Switzerland

Preface

This volume contains the proceedings of the ICWE 2016 Rapid Mashup Challenge (http://challenge.webengineering.org) that was held on June 6, 2016, in Lugano, Switzerland, in conjunction with the 16th International Conference on Web Engineering (ICWE, http://icwe2016.webengineering.org). The 2016 edition of the challenge is the second instalment of a series of challenges that aim to engage researchers and practitioners in a competition for the best mashup approach.

The contributions printed in this volume are post-challenge extensions of the short participation proposals the authors prepared to express their interest in participating in the challenge and that the organizers of the challenge used to select participants based on the interest and maturity of the proposals. The original short versions of the contributions are available online in the program section of the challenge: http://challenge. webengineering.org/program/.

We would like to thank the authors for their excellent work before and after the challenge as well as for their commitment and engagement during the challenge itself. The presented tools and approaches are of course the core of the event and of this volume. We also would like to thank the audience for participating and the Program Committee members for helping us assure the quality of the post-workshop proceedings printed in this volume. Of course, we would also like to thank Springer, especially Aliaksandr Birukou, for promoting and printing the proceedings of the challenge in their CCIS series. This allowed us once again to provide a complete picture of the proposals the challenge attracted, without having to be too strict with the acceptance of contributions in the first place and allowing us to work together with the authors on their contributions in the post-challenge phase.

We are grateful to everyone who contributed to this volume and confident the reader will find the reading interesting, inspiring, and – hopefully – also challenging.

September 2016
Florian Daniel
Martin Gaedke

Organization

Program Committee

Saeed Aghaee	University of Cambridge, UK
Christoph Bussler	Oracle Corporation, USA
Cinzia Cappiello	Politecnico di Milano, Italy
Sven Casteleyn	Universitat Jaume I, Spain
Oscar Diaz	University of the Basque Country, Spain
Agnes Koschmider	Karlsruhe Institute of Technology, Germany
Maristella Matera	Politecnico di Milano, Italy
Tommi Mikkonen	Tampere University of Technology, Finland
Cesare Pautasso	University of Lugano, Switzerland
Victoria Torres	Universidad Politécnica de Valencia, Spain
Tomas Vitvar	Czech Technical University, Czech Republic
Michael Weiss	Carleton University, Canada

Contents

ICWE 2016 Rapid Mashup Challenge: Introduction

Florian Daniel[1(✉)] and Martin Gaedke[2]

[1] Politecnico di Milano, Via Ponzio 34/5, 20133 Milano, Italy
`florian.daniel@polimi.it`
[2] Technische Universität Chemnitz, Str. der Nationen 62, 09111 Chemnitz, Germany
`martin.gaedke@informatik.tu-chemnitz.de`

Abstract. The ICWE 2016 Rapid Mashup Challenge is the second installment of a series of challenges that aim to engage researchers and practitioners in showcasing and discussing their work on assisting mashup development. This introduction provides the reader with the general context of the Challenge, its objectives and motivation, and the requirements contributions were asked to satisfy so as to be eligible for participation. A summary of the contributions that were selected for presentation in the 2016 edition anticipates the content of the remainder of this volume.

Keywords: Mashups · Mashup tools · Challenge · Benchmarking

1 Context and Objective

Mashups, that is "composite applications developed starting from reusable data, application logic and/or user interfaces typically, but not mandatorily, sourced from the Web" [1], have been the subject of research and industrial study for several years by now. Over the same time span, we also witnessed an iterative specialization of the term: while in the beginning all types of applications developed by reusing resources from the Web were referred to as "mashups," today – also thanks to the pioneering efforts by the mashup community – this kind of integration of Web-accessible resources has become common practice in software engineering and can, hence, no longer be considered a practice that is easy to isolate from software engineering in general. Today, the term is instead more focused on those applications that are developed with the help from a so-called *mashup tool* (possibly ranging from full-fledged integrated development environments to dedicated programming libraries) that aims to ease mashup development via suitable abstractions and automations. Thanks to the respective simplified development processes, often mashups are further associated with *end users* that not necessarily possess programming knowledge but that nevertheless may want to or be required to develop own situational applications, e.g., to automate tasks in their everyday business.

In line with last year's edition [2], the ICWE 2016 Rapid Mashup Challenge[1] acknowledges this peculiarity of mashups and puts its focus on the techniques,

---

[1] http://challenge.webengineering.org/.

© Springer International Publishing AG 2017
F. Daniel and M. Gaedke (Eds.): RMC 2016, CCIS 696, pp. 1–9, 2017.
DOI: 10.1007/978-3-319-53174-8_1

approaches, libraries, and tools that researchers and practitioners have come up with so far to aid the development of mashups – to all types of users and/or programmers. This perspective is different from the perspectives of similar challenges known from other contexts or communities. For instance, the Semantic Web Challenge[2] focuses on the application of Semantic Web [3] technologies in the development of software with commercial potential, large user bases, or functionality that is useful and of societal value. The AI Mashup Challenge[3], instead, more specifically focuses on mashups that use AI (Artificial Intelligence) technology (e.g., machine learning and data mining, machine vision, natural language processing, reasoning, ontologies) and intelligence to mashup existing resources. The Rapid Mashup Challenge, instead, does not limit its focus to any specific technology and rather aims to understand how mashups can be developed, independently of how their internals look like.

The purpose of the Challenge is further that of comparing the proposed development approaches with each other, so as to stimulate the interchange of ideas among researchers and practitioners and to cross-fertilize them. Yet, objectively comparing approaches that are as diverse as mashup approaches is a hard endeavor. In fact, while last year we used (i) an explicit feature checklist to be filled by authors to assess the expressive power of the proposed approaches and (ii) a common mashup development scenario to assess the elegance and ease of development, this year we decided to leave proponents more freedom in showcasing their approach and did not impose any specific development scenario. The reason for this choice is that the proposals we received this year[4] were characterized by very diverse levels of maturity, ranging from production-ready instruments to proof-of-concept prototypes. Requiring all of them to support one and a same development scenario would have meant precluding the less mature approaches from participating, as they simply would not have been able to provide the necessary development support to implement a full-fledged mashup. Since we however felt that also the less mature works proposed ideas and solutions that had merits and deserved presentation, we opted for a less rigorous comparison in favor of more variety and a better representation of the latest state of the art in mashup development assistance.

In the following, we summarize the structure of the Challenge and the feature checklist. Then we briefly introduce the approaches that were selected for presentation in the 2016 edition of the Challenge, while the papers in the remainder of this volume (extensions of the initial participation proposals) explain each of the approaches in more detail and describe the respective demonstrations given live during the Challenge.

2   Structure of Challenge

The Challenge was again organized into four phases:

---

1. **Admission:** Submission of applications. Each application had to include a brief description of the proposed tool/approach and a filled feature checklist, so as to allow the organizers to pre-select proposals based on topic and interestingness.
2. **Preparation:** If a proposal was accepted to the challenge, the authors could use the time from the notification till the Challenge to prepare an as effective as possible demonstration of their approach. This preparation phase gave the authors almost six weeks to prepare for the event.
3. **Competition:** During the Challenge, participants had to give both a presentation and a live demonstration of how to build a mashup – both within a maximum of 20 min. Last year, we strictly limited the time of the live demonstration to 10 min, giving all participants the same time for the development of a same mashup. Since this year we did without the reference mashup, we allowed participants to use their time as best as they felt.
4. **Post-challenge:** Preparation of post-challenge paper explaining the proposed solution and giving technical details about the approach and how it was used to rapidly build their demonstration mashup.

The goal of this structure is to have authors focus more on the practical aspects before the Challenge (the preparation of their demonstration), while asking them to concentrate on the conceptual and scientific aspects afterwards (with the writing of the paper to be included in this volume).

3   Feature Checklist

In order to facilitate the comparison of approaches, authors were required to accompany their submission with a filled feature checklist that describes the two key parts of the evaluation, i.e., the nature of the mashups that their tool/approach allows one to develop and the development features of the proposed tool. The following subsections describe the features in more detail.

3.1   Mashup Features

In order to be able to compare the mashups produced by the different approaches during the Challenge, the mashup features proposed by Daniel and Matera [1] were taken as reference:

- **Mashup type:** The mashup type expresses the positioning of the mashup at one or more of the three layers of the typical application stack (data, logic, presentation), depending on where the mashup's integration logic is positioned. *Data mashups* operate at the data layer, integrate data sources, and are typically published again as data sources (e.g., RSS feeds or RESTful Web services). *Logic mashups* integrate components at the application logic layer, reuse data and application logic (e.g., Web services), and are typically published as Web services. *User Interface (UI) mashups* are located at the presentation layer, integrate UI components/widgets, and are published as Web applications that users can interact with via the Web browser. Finally, *hybrid mashups* span multiple layers of the application stack.

- **Component types:** The types of mashups introduced above strongly relate to the types of the components they integrate. *Data components* comprise RSS and Atom feeds, XML, JSON, CSV and similar data resources, web data extractions, micro-formats, but also SOAP or RESTful web services that are used as data services only. *Logic components* comprise SOAP and RESTful web services, JavaScript APIs and libraries, device APIs, and API extractions. *UI components* comprise code snippets and JavaScript UI libraries, Java portlets, widgets and gadgets, web clips and extracted UI components.
- **Runtime location:** There are generally a variety of possible architectural configurations that may be adopted for the development of mashups, compatibly with the requirements of the chosen components. *Client-side* mashups are executed in the client browser. *Server-side* mashups are executed in the server. *Client-server* mashups are distributed over client and server, and both parts interact the one with the other at runtime.
- **Integration logic:** The integration logic tells how integration happens, that is, how components are used to form a composite application and how they are enabled to communicate with each other (if at all). *UI-based integration* applies exclusively to UI components and uses the graphical layout of the mashup's user interface to render UI components in parallel next to each other inside one or more web pages. *Orchestrated integration* applies to all kinds of components and consists in a centralized composition logic. *Choreographed integration* is for all those types of components that are able to comply with a given convention (oftentimes also called a contract or protocol), so as to manage integration without a central coordinator.
- **Instantiation lifecycle:** The last aspect of mashups considered is how long an instantiated mashup is running. *Stateless mashups* do not require keeping any internal state for their execution and end after processing. *Short-living* mashups are mashups that last the time of a user session, i.e., as long as a user is interacting with the mashup in the client browser, and terminate with the closing of the client browser. *Long-living* mashups may last longer than a user session, that is, they survive even after the user closes the browser with the rendered mashup or after the first invocation of the mashup.

These five features allow one to easily classify mashups and to assess their internal complexity. Of course, this is not an exhaustive list of characteristics and many other distinguishing features could be examined [1]. Yet, for the sake of assessing the suitability and interestingness of approaches we considered these five features as enough.

3.2   Mashup Tool Features

The comparison of the features of the mashup tools/approaches was instead based on the work by Aghaee et al. [4].

- **Targeted end-user:** Determining which group of users is targeted by a mashup tool/approach is a strategic design issue decided by the developers. *Non-programmers* do not have programming skills. Yet, they may be interested in creating mashups as long as it does not require them to learn and use a programming language. *Local developers* are those non-programmers who usually have advanced knowledge in computer tools. *Expert programmers* have adequate programming skills and experience to develop mashups using programming and scripting languages (e.g., JavaScript and PHP).
- **Automation degree:** The automation degree of a mashup tool refers to how much of the development process can be undertaken by the tool on behalf of its users. *Full automation* of mashup development eliminates the need for direct involvement of users in the development process. *Semi-automatic* tools partially automate mashup development by providing guidance and assistance. *Manual* approaches do not provide any automated support during development; typically, these approaches come in the form of programming libraries or runtime middlewares.
- **Liveness level:** Tanimoto proposed the concept of liveness [5], according to which four levels of liveness can be distinguished. At *Level 1* (non-executable prototype mockup), a tool is just used to create prototype mashups that are not directly connected to any kind of run-time system. *Level 2* (explicit compilation and deployment steps) of liveness is characterized by mashup design blueprints that carry sufficient details to give them an executable semantics. *Level 3* (automatic compilation and deployment) tools support rapid deployment into operation, e.g., triggered by each edit-change or by an explicit action executed by the developer. *Level 4* (dynamic modification of running mashup) of mashup liveness is obtained by the tools that support live modification of the mashup code, while it is being executed.
- **Interaction technique:** There have been a number of interaction techniques through the use of which the barriers of programming can be lifted to its developers [6]. *Editable examples* let users modify and change the behavior of existing examples, instead of programming from scratch. In *form-based* interaction, users are asked to fill out a form to create a new or change the behavior of an existing object. *Programming by demonstration* suggests to teach a computer by example how to accomplish a particular task. *Spreadsheets* are one of the most popular and widely used end-user programming approaches to store, manipulate, and display complex data. *Textual DSLs* are languages targeted to address specific problems in a particular domain; they have a textual syntax that may or may not resemble an existing general-purpose programming language. A *visual language* (iconic), as opposed to a textual programming language, is any programming language that uses visual symbols, syntax, and semantics. Some visual languages support *wiring with implicit control flow*, where the control flow of the mashup is derived from its data flow graph. Other visual languages support *wiring with explicit control flow*, where the control flow is explicitly defined, for instance, by adding directed arrows connecting the boxes, or putting the boxes in a specific order (e.g., from left to right). *WYSIWYG* (What You See Is What You Get) enables users to create

and modify a mashup on a graphical user interface that is similar to the one that will appear when the mashup runs. *Natural language* allows developers to express their mashup via a restricted, controlled set of natural language constructs (e.g., a subset of English) that can be interpreted unequivocally by a runtime environment.

- **Online user community:** Online communities are an important resource in assisting developers, especially end-users, to program [7]. If a tool does not support any online community (*none*), it is harder to leverage on the experience of others. In *public* communities, the content is accessible to any user on the Web who wishes to join the community (with or without registration). In *private* communities, the authority to join the community is granted on the basis of compliance with some operator-specified criteria.

Like for the mashup features, also in the case of the mashup tools/approaches many other characteristics could be considered (e.g., collaboration). The features selected for the Challenge, however, already provide good insight into the philosophy behind each approach, and we preferred to keep the list concise.

4   Participants

The following contributions were selected for participation in the Challenge[5]:

- *FlexMash 2.0 – Flexible Modeling and Execution of Data Mashups* by Pascal Hirmer and Michael Behringer: FlexMash is a data mashup tool that aims at facilitating the integration and processing of heterogeneous, dynamic data sources. It targets domain experts, features a graphical pipes and filter modeling paradigm, and supports the enforcement of non-functional requirements like security and robustness. The first version of the tool was presented during the 2015 edition of the Challenge; the new version comes with cloud-based execution and human interaction during runtime.
- *The SmartComposition Approach for Creating Environment-Aware Multi-screen Mashups* by Michael Krug, Fabian Wiedemann, Markus Ast and Martin Gaedke: The SmartComposition approach is a UI mashup framework that supports local developers (non-experts) in creating environment-aware multi-screen mashups by leveraging on HTML markup only. Supported Web components can range from data sources to components that provide access to the Web of Things, e.g., to control actuators and access sensors. Mashup execution across multiple screens is enabled using a messaging service based on WebSockets.
- *Linked Widgets Platform for Rapid Collaborative Semantic Mashup Development* by Tuan-Dat Trinh, Ba-Lam Do, Peter Wetz, Peb Ruswono Aryan,

---

[5] We would like to thank Michael Luggen and Eduard Daoud for participating in the Challenge with their presentations of, respectively, the Uduvudu Editor and search-based mashup development. It's a pity that, due to time constraints, we were not able to include a long version of their proposals in these post-challenge proceedings.

Elmar Kiesling and A Min Tjoa: The Linked Widgets platforms is a mashup platform that combines the Semantic Web and mashups to help users integrate data and make informed decisions in decision making processes. The tool is based on a semantic model of mashup components that enables the automation of some typical data integration tasks, such as overcoming data heterogeneity and data exploration. In addition, the Linked Widgets platform supports a live, collaborative mashup development and execution model able to easily bring together multiple stakeholders.

– *End-User Development for the Internet of Things: EFESTO and the 5Ws composition paradigm* by Giuseppe Desolda, Carmelo Ardito and Maristella Matera: EFESTO is another tool that was presented as well in 2015. This new version comes with a novel rule-based composition paradigm (exhibiting similarities with the well-known IFTTT) that provides also for the composition of so-called smart objects, i.e., components that encapsulate sensors and/or actuators accessible via the Internet of Things. The described work targets end-users via a dedicated visual rule composition notation.

– *Toolet: an editor for Web-based tool appropriation by hobby programmers* by Jeremías P. Contell and Oscar Díaz: Toolet is an editor for Web appropriation, that is, for the ad-hoc adaptation of third-party Web applications to the needs of users performed by the users themselves. The level of abstraction to enable users to integrate and manipulate data proposed by Toolet is an original one based on Google Spreadsheets. The adaptation of Web applications is then based on Web augmentation techniques, which also cater for hobby programmers. Toolet is one of the early prototypes included in this volume.

– *On the Role of Context in the Design of Mobile Mashups* by Valerio Cassani, Stefano Gianelli, Maristella Matera, Riccardo Medana, Elisa Quintarelli, Letizia Tanca and Vittorio Zaccaria: This contribution introduced CAMUS, a design methodology and an accompanying platform for the design and fast development of Context-Aware Mobile mashUpS. The approach revolves around the concept of context to effectively cater to situational needs of users, while the target mashups are mobile applications. Internally the platform makes use of adaptable model-driven engineering techniques. The presented tool is an early prototype of the envisioned platform.

Table 1 summarizes the characteristics of the selected approaches as declared by the authors. Compared to last year, it is evident that the Internet of Things has percolated into the presented approaches, and most of the proposals aim at supporting hybrid mashups, featuring integration logics stemming from the data, logic and UI layers. The strong focus on end-users without significant programming skills is confirmed also this year, as is – in line with this observation – the focus on graphical development paradigms (ranging from editable examples to iconic and WYSIWYG paradigms) and dynamic, live (level 4) and automatic (level 3) development approaches.

Together, this selection of mashup approaches provides an intriguing snapshot of the current state of the art in research on mashup development aids. Some proposals are already very mature and close to production systems

Table 1. Overview of the mashup and mashup tool features declared by the approaches that participated in the ICWE 2016 Rapid Mashup Challenge.

			FlexMash 2.0	SmartComposition	Linked Widgets	Toolet	EFESTO	CAMUS
Mashup	**Mashup type**	Data mashups	✓				✓	✓
		Logic mashups						
		UI mashups						✓
		Hybrid mashups		✓	✓	✓		
	Component types	Data components	✓	✓	✓	✓	✓	✓
		Logic components		✓	✓	✓	✓	✓
		UI components		✓	✓	✓		✓
	Runtime location	Client-side only				✓		
		Server-side only					✓	
		Client-server	✓	✓	✓			✓
	Integration logic	UI-based integr.						
		Orchestration	✓		✓	✓	✓	✓
		Choreography		✓	✓			
	Instantiation lifecycle	Stateless	✓					
		Short-living		✓	✓			
		Long-living			✓	✓	✓	✓
Mashup tool	**Target end-user**	Local developers		✓			✓	✓
		Non-programmers	✓		✓			
		Expert programmers				✓		
	Automation degree	Full automation			✓			✓
		Semi-automation	✓		✓	✓	✓	
		Manual		✓	✓			
	Liveness level	Level 1 (mockup)						
		Level 2 (manual)				✓		
		Level 3 (automatic)	✓		✓			✓
		Level 4 (dynamic)		✓			✓	
	Interaction technique	Editable examples		✓				
		Form-based				✓		
		Progr. by demonstration						
		Spreadsheets				✓		
		Textual DSL						
		Visual (iconic)	✓				✓	✓
		Visual (wiring, implicit)			✓			
		Visual (wiring, explicit)				✓		
		WYSIWYG						✓
		Natural language						
	Online user community	None	✓	✓		✓	✓	✓
		Private						
		Public			✓			

(e.g., FlexMash 2.0, SmartComposition, Linked Widgets, search-based mashups, and EFESTO), while others are still in an early stage of development (e.g., Toolet and CAMUS). Yet, they all provide good insight into the research questions and technological trends researchers are intrigued by right now and that still ask for good questions before we can say that mashup development is properly assisted for all kinds of target developers.

We are confident that the reader will find the remainder of this volume, which provides detailed insight into the introduced approaches, as intriguing as we do.

References

1. Daniel, F., Matera, M.: Mashups: Concepts, Models and Architectures. Springer, Heidelberg (2014)
2. Daniel, F., Pautasso, C. (eds.): Rapid Mashup Development Tools. CCIS, vol. 591. Springer, Heidelberg (2016)
3. Berners-Lee, T., Hendler, J., Lassila, O.: The semantic web. Sci. Am. **284**, 34–43 (2001)
4. Aghaee, S., Nowak, M., Pautasso, C.: Reusable decision space for mashup tool design. In: Barbosa, S.D.J., Campos, J.C., Kazman, R., Palanque, P.A., Harrison, M.D., Reeves, S., (eds.): EICS, pp. 211–220. ACM (2012)
5. Tanimoto, S.L.: Viva: a visual language for image processing. J. Vis. Lang. Comput. **1**(2), 127–139 (1990)
6. Myers, B.A., Ko, A.J., Burnett, M.M.: Invited research overview: end-user programming. In: CHI 2006 Extended Abstracts on Human Factors in Computing Systems, pp. 75–80. ACM (2006)
7. Nardi, B.A.: A Small Matter of Programming: Perspectives on End User Computing. MIT Press, Cambridge (1993)

FlexMash 2.0 – Flexible Modeling and Execution of Data Mashups

Pascal Hirmer$^{(\boxtimes)}$ and Michael Behringer

Institute of Parallel and Distributed Systems, University of Stuttgart,
Universitätsstraße 38, 70569 Stuttgart, Germany
{pascal.hirmer,michael.behringer}@ipvs.uni-stuttgart.de

Abstract. In recent years, the amount of data highly increases through cheap hardware, fast network technology, and the increasing digitization within most domains. The data produced is oftentimes heterogeneous, dynamic and originates from many highly distributed data sources. Deriving information and, as a consequence, knowledge from this data can lead to a higher effectiveness for problem solving and thus higher profits for companies. However, this is a great challenge – oftentimes referred to as Big Data problem. The data mashup tool FlexMash, developed at the University of Stuttgart, tackles this challenge by offering a means for integration and processing of heterogeneous, dynamic data sources. By doing so, FlexMash focuses on (i) an easy means to model data integration and processing scenarios by domain-experts based on the Pipes and Filters pattern, (ii) a flexible execution based on the user's non-functional requirements, and (iii) high extensibility to enable a generic approach. A first version of this tool was presented during the ICWE Rapid Mashup Challenge 2015. In this article, we present the new version FlexMash 2.0, which introduces new features such as cloud-based execution and human interaction during runtime. These concepts have been presented during the ICWE Rapid Mashup Challenge 2016.

Keywords: ICWE Rapid Mashup Challenge 2016 · FlexMash · Data processing and integration · Pipes and Filters

1 Context and Goals

Today, data becomes more and more important throughout all domains. Especially the integration and processing of a large amount of distributed data sources can lead to valuable knowledge, which e.g., enables higher profits for companies due to an increased efficiency and effectiveness for problem solving. Oftentimes, this valuable knowledge can only be derived based on a large number of data sources, which is a great challenge. A common way to cope with this challenge are Extract-Transform-Load (ETL) processes. However, traditional ETL processes have several shortcomings: (i) they are very complex and require a lot of effort for creation, (ii) they require deep technical knowledge about the data, algorithms and technology, and (iii) they are oftentimes executed in a static execution

© Springer International Publishing AG 2017
F. Daniel and M. Gaedke (Eds.): RMC 2016, CCIS 696, pp. 10–29, 2017.
DOI: 10.1007/978-3-319-53174-8_2

environment, which can only cope with specific requirements. In our previous work [7,9] we introduced FlexMash, a data mashup tool that copes with these issues by (i) enabling a fast creation of data integration and processing scenarios without the definition of complex ETL processes, by (ii) domain-specific modeling based on the Pipes and Filters patterns, which enables usage by users without deep technical knowledge, and by (iii) a flexible execution based on the non-functional requirements of the users (such as security, robustness, efficiency), which leads to a tailor-made execution for each user. Furthermore, FlexMash enables an ad-hoc and explorative approach for data processing. Through easy adaptations of the abstracted model, desired results can be achieved in a step-wise manner. For example, new data sources can be added easily to improve the results without any programming effort.

In this article, we present the new version FlexMash 2.0, which offers enhanced features to further improve the solution provided by the first version of FlexMash. Among improvements regarding the usability and the frontend as well as efficiency improvements of the backend, we introduce two new concepts, which are enhancing FlexMash 2.0: (i) automated deployment of data mashups in distributed cloud computing environments, and (ii) extending data mashups with human interaction during runtime. We will describe these concepts in this article. Furthermore, we will describe the preparation and the demonstration of the FlexMash 2.0 tool during the ICWE Rapid Mashup Challenge. By doing so, we will describe the scenario we prepared for the demo and also challenges we encountered during preparation.

The remainder of this article is structured as follows: In Sect. 2, we describe basic concepts that are necessary to comprehend the approach of this article. Section 3 introduces the main contribution of this article by introducing Flex-Mash 2.0 – flexible execution and modeling of data mashups. After that, Sects. 4, 5 and 6 describe details regarding the tool demonstration at the Rapid Mashup Challenge 2016, including the tool's features, its level of maturity, and the demo scenario that was presented. In Sect. 7, we describe related work. Finally, Sect. 8 gives a summary and an outlook on future work.

2 Basic Concepts

This section introduces important concepts that serve as foundation for this article.

2.1 Data Mashup Modeling and Processing Based on Pipes and Filters

The design pattern *Pipes and Filters* [13] is well-established for building modular, highly extensible applications and inspired many application and mashup modeling approaches. The basic idea of this pattern is to create software components (the filters), also referred to as services or micro-services, that offer

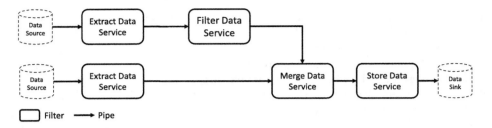

Fig. 1. Basic example of Pipes and Filters based data processing

uniform interfaces (e.g., REST) and are based on a uniform data exchange format. This enables an easy interconnection of these services through so called pipes – the connections between the filters. An example for a Pipes and Filter based data processing approach is depicted in Fig. 1.

The idea of Pipes and Filters has been adopted in many data mashup approaches. In FlexMash, we also build on the concepts of the Pipes and Filters pattern both on the modeling level and on the execution level. This means, the modeler of the data mashup first creates a graphical model such as the one depicted in Fig. 1, which is called *Mashup Plan* in the context of FlexMash. After that, this model is transformed into an executable format such as, e.g., a workflow model. The functionality of the filters is provided by services that are called in the order as defined by the data mashup model. Due to the fact that each service has uniform interfaces and works based on the same data exchange format, we can easily interconnect them arbitrarily.

2.2   TOSCA

The OASIS standard Topology and Orchestration Specification for Cloud Applications (TOSCA) provides a means for automated application provisioning in cloud computing environments and for their management. To enable this means, the topology of an application has to be provided in a model called Service Template. This model contains specific information about all the components of an application ranging from infrastructure to platforms to software components. As a consequence, TOSCA unifies the cloud computing paradigms infrastructure as a service, platform as a service and software as a service. Each component is represented in the topology as so called Node Template, the connections between components are represented by so called Relationship Templates. Node and Relationship Templates are typed by Node Types and Relationship Types, respectively. Furthermore, these templates can be attached with a list of properties and so called Implementation Artifacts, which contain scripts or binaries to provision and manage the component. The topology model can then be used for application provisioning using a TOSCA runtime environment. Though, in this case, the runtime has to work in a declarative manner, which means that it contains explicit knowledge about the modeled components and can set them up

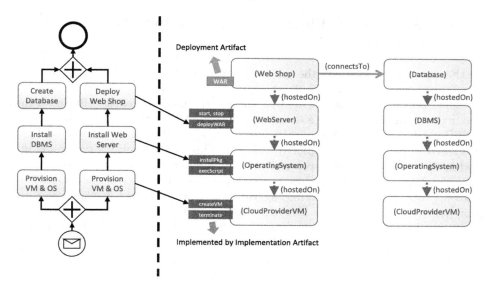

Fig. 2. Example of a TOSCA Build Plan (left) and a TOSCA application topology (right)

in the right order solely based on the topology model. However, most TOSCA runtimes do not support such a declarative approach, and thus are more generic, i.e., they are able to provision and manage arbitrary applications not only the ones known to the runtime. This is referred to as an imperative approach. To enable this, an additional artifact has to be provided with the topology. This artifact is called the Build Plan, oftentimes also referred to as Provisioning Plan. The Plan specifies exactly how and in which order the components have to be set up. For example, an application server container has to be set up first before a web application can be deployed into it. An example for a TOSCA topology and a corresponding provisioning plan is depicted in Fig. 2. In this example, a web shop application connected to a database is modeled and can be provisioned automatically by executing the Build Plan. In this article, we use the concepts of TOSCA to automatically deploy data mashups in distributed cloud computing environments to enable scalability, availability and saving costs. By doing so, we use a combination of an imperative and declarative approach, which is enabled through the TOSCA Build Plan generator as described in [4]. Our prototype shown in the demo of the Rapid Mashup Challenge is implemented based on the open-source TOSCA runtime environment OpenTOSCA.

The open source ecosystem *OpenTOSCA* [3] includes a graphical modeling tool called *Winery* [12] and a plan-based provisioning and management runtime environment, which can be used to provision and manage TOSCA applications fully automatically. The interested reader is referred to the official OASIS TOSCA specification [14], TOSCA Primer [15], or Binz et al. [2].

3 FlexMash 2.0 – Flexible Execution and Modeling of Data Mashups

In this section, we describe the main concepts of FlexMash and we show how they have been extended in contrast to previous work.

The FlexMash approach is applied through the method depicted in Fig. 3. In the first step of this method, a domain-user without any extensive programming skills models a so called Mashup Plan, a Pipes and Filters based flow model as described in Sect. 2.1 and depicted in Fig. 4. This model contains two kinds of nodes: (i) Data Source Description (DSD) nodes describing the data sources that hold the data, and (ii) Data Processing Description (DPD) nodes that describe data operations for, e.g., filtering, aggregation, data analytics, visualization or storage. As described in Sect. 2.1, these nodes can be interconnected arbitrarily due to the fact that they have the same interfaces and the same data interchange format as defined by the Pipes and Filters pattern. The model depicted in Fig. 4

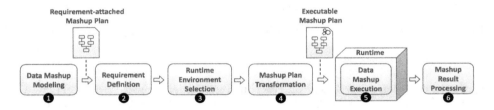

Fig. 3. The FlexMash method (based on [8])

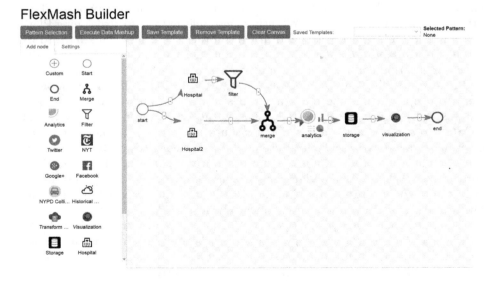

Fig. 4. Data Mashup modeling in FlexMash

gives an example for such a Mashup Plan. In this scenario, data from two different hospitals are being integrated and analytics is conducted based on the result. We assume that these hospitals store similar data, however, there are differences, e.g., one of the hospitals contains additional information that are not important for the integrated result. This information should be removed through a filter before merging. To realize this scenario, this model contains two Data Source Descriptions for the hospitals, as well as five Data Processing Descriptions for filtering, merging, analytics, storage, and visualization. Through interconnection of these nodes, this and many other scenarios can be realized using the FlexMash approach. Note that all technical details, e.g., the concrete data structure of the hospitals are abstracted, the modeler only needs to know which data is stored and not how it is stored.

After modeling, in step 2 of this method, the modeler selects non-functional requirements from the *requirement catalog* depicted in Fig. 5. This catalog contains a textual description of supported non-functional requirements containing a problem description, a provided solution, how the requirement can be fulfilled, an evaluation, and information about how the requirement can be combined with others. These descriptions are kept as free as possible from technical details so domain users can understand them and select them appropriately. Examples for non-functional requirements are robustness, security, or efficiency. Furthermore, a means is provided to combine several requirements with each other. However, some combinations have to be restricted such as robustness and efficiency. The requirements will be used to provide a tailor-made execution for each modeler that fits their specific use cases and scenarios. Note that the requirement catalog currently serves as informative service and does not provide any selection suggestions based on the modeled Mashup Plan. This is part of our future work.

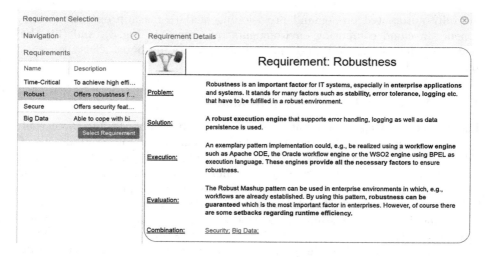

Fig. 5. Selection of non-functional requirements in a requirement catalog

In step 3, a runtime environment is selected suitable for the requirements defined in step 2. This means that software components are put together in a modular manner depending on the combination of requirements. For example, a robust execution would also require an execution engine that provides features such as error handling or rollbacks. These software components are retrieved by the graph algorithm described in [7]. This algorithm returns a list of software components that are suitable to fulfill the selected non-functional requirements. This list serves as basis for the mashup execution. In previous work, we assume that all possible software components to run the data mashup are already set up. In this article, we show how these components can be set up on-demand and fully automatically (cf. Sect. 3.2). Common engines used for mashup execution are workflow engines that, e.g., execute BPEL workflows to invoke services that process and integrate the data.

In step 4, the non-executable Mashup Plan that was modeled in step 1 is transformed into an executable representation appropriate for the selected runtime environment (e.g., into a BPEL workflow). To realize this, several mappings are provided that transform the abstract generic Mashup Plans into concrete, executable models. The data operations and data sources to be executed by the mashup are encapsulated into services (e.g., Java web services) that are then being invoked by the executable model.

In step 5, the transformed executable representation of the Mashup Plan is executed in the appropriate engine. This engine invokes services to extract and process data in the order defined by the Mashup Plan.

Finally, in step 6, the result can be used for visualization in dashboards, analysis or further value-adding scenarios.

The presented method has been enhanced and improved with additional features that have been presented the first time at the ICWE Rapid Mashup Challenge 2016. Those are (i) the concept of sub-flows on the modeling level, (ii) the fully automated on-demand provisioning of data mashup execution components in cloud computing environments (cf. step 3 in Fig. 3), and (iii) the enabling of human interaction during runtime of data mashups. Those concepts are described in the following.

3.1 Subflows for Data Mashup Modeling

The first new concept we present are subflows. Subflows are Mashup Plans that can be used for modeling within other Mashup Plans. By doing so, all details of the subflow are hidden into a single node. This makes modeling a lot easier, and, furthermore, enhances the reusability of Mashup Plans. Experts could define often recurring patterns and model them as subflows. For example, the extraction and filtering of data from a SQL database is a very common pattern that is modeled many times in different Mashup Plans. As a consequence, it makes sense to provide this Mashup Plan as a pattern to be reused by others. Furthermore, we enable a conservation of knowledge. This means that experienced users can model recurring scenarios and can provide them, e.g. to their colleagues, through subflow nodes. This can save a lot of effort and can further reduce necessary expertise when modeling the Mashup Plan. An example for a subflow is depicted in Fig. 6.

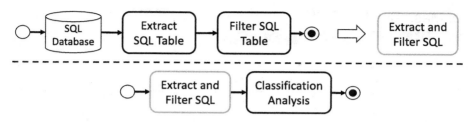

Fig. 6. Top: transformation from a Mashup Plan into a subflow node. Bottom: exemplary usage of a subflow node

3.2 On-Demand Provisioning of Data Mashup Execution Components

As depicted in Fig. 3, the execution environment is selected in step 3 of the introduced method based on the non-functional requirements of the users. In previous work, we assumed that all components that could be used for mashup execution are up and running. However, this leads to high costs due to an extensive use of resources. Especially some components are rarely used so it does not make sense to keep them running at all times. We further extend the FlexMash method to provide a means for automated, on-demand setup and execution of software components based on the Topology Orchestration Specification for Cloud Applications (TOSCA) that was introduced in Sect. 2.2.

After step 3 of our method, the selection of a suitable runtime environment for the data mashup execution, we receive a list of necessary components. These components should be set up automatically and only when they are needed for mashup execution. Based on the information provided on the list, a TOSCA topology template is created automatically using the topology completion algorithm provided in [6]. Furthermore, through the plan generator extension provided by [4], we are able to generate the TOSCA build plan based on the completed topology. This topology is then used for automated setup of data mashup execution components such as workflow engines, databases for storing intermediate results, and services for executing data operations. Detailed information about this step is provided in [8].

3.3 Extending Data Mashups with Interactivity

(Data) Mashups are a proven approach for special solutions by providing a great advantage for a small number of users, whose demand is not considered important enough for a prefabricated application [5]. The user is therefore able to build a customized solution based on his requirements with reduced technical knowledge required. Unfortunately, most applications still require an extensive knowledge of the processes and parameters used and for this reason are not adaptable for the ordinary domain experts to use.

It is undisputed that interactive elements provide several advantages, such as a deeper understanding of the characteristics of the data to be analyzed and as a

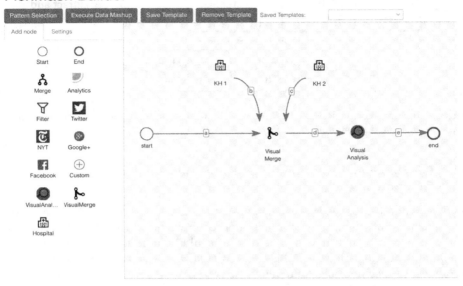

Fig. 7. Use case: health analytics

consequence, better and more accurate results as shown in different user studies (e.g., Savikhin et al. [16]). Another major advantage is the possibility to make use of the implicit domain knowledge of a user during the analysis process [18]. These advantages are, however, paid for with a partial loss of objectivity and velocity. The former can cause a problem if the user wants to prove a particular hypothesis and ignores obvious patterns in the data because they do not meet the objective [17]. The latter is unavoidable when involving the user, as this always requires more time than an automated process. Consequently, it must be considered for each use case whether the involvement of the user offers required advantages, however, in many cases an advantage is expectable. Nonetheless most applications are, regarding interactivity, limited to the modeling of workflows and specifying different parameters through a graphical user interface.

In the following section, we introduce a prototypical Data Processing Description that can be used for modeling in Mashup Plans, which allows interactive merging of different data sources under full control of the user – the Visual Merge Node. This concept is based on the work of Kandel et al. [10], but with a strong focus on the specific requirements of Data Mashups and the associated integration of multiple data sources. For evaluation purposes, we used a test data set with generated values of a fictional health care scenario. The modeled use case is depicted in Fig. 7. This scenario describes the analysis of two health data sets from two different hospitals, but is also applicable for a higher number of data sources. This data sources have been previously added to FlexMash by a technical expert and placed in the modeled scenario by a domain expert through drag

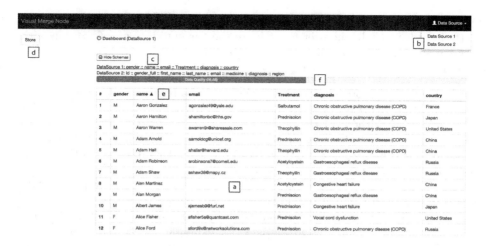

Fig. 8. Visual merge node

and drop, describing the input data for our new Visual Merge Node, which is described in detail later in this section. Furthermore there is a placeholder called Visual Analysis Node depicted, which is not described in detail in this article. Both hospital sources offering a JSON-file describing patient data like name, gender, illness and optionally a diagnosis and different contact information. The exercise for the domain expert is to convert the initial two heterogeneous data sources into a combined homogeneous one by controlling every step of the data integration over an intuitive user interface.

The graphical user interface is depicted in Fig. 8 and consists of different components:

Data Table – The main component of the user interface is a central data table (a) used for displaying the contents of the incoming JSON file.

Data Source-Switch – Due to the unknown number of data sources to be coped with, we implemented a menu for switching the actively displayed data source (b).

Schema Integration – Incoming data could be of very different characteristic, therefore we provide an optional menu showing the differences in schemata (c), which allows the user to evaluate attribute accordance between data sources.

Proceed Workflow – The user can continue execution (d) of the modeled workflow, once the objective quality is sufficient. Furthermore, the continuation of the processing is possible until an adequate subjective quality is achieved. The current record is then converted to the standard data exchange format for FlexMash.

Sorting – Naturally, the user interface offers simple sorting capabilities (e) allowing different views of the record.

Quality Meter – A quality measurement meter is visualized on top of the table (f) in order to help the user to evaluate the current state of integration with a single view. This quality measure is by now based on schema coincidence and empty values.

The presented prototype node provides several advantages over the previous merge-functionality. Previously, it was necessary to specify the exact attribute for a join operation without the possibility for further optimization of the records. With the new Visual Merge Node there is no need to know anything about join operations, it is an intuitive and iterative process under full control of the user. Furthermore, not all semantic errors could be automatically identified [11] and human interaction is needed to eliminate them. For this reason an improved data quality is expected if the user is involved in the analysis process.

As conclusion, it can be stated that the integration of domain experts during mashup execution has many advantages, for example the inclusion of implicit background knowledge, the recognition and correction of additional semantic errors, an increase of the understanding of the data set and a better selection of data for analysis. There is a great potential by integrating the domain expert not only in the final analysis but also in each step of the Mashup Plan. Nevertheless it must be noted that the user can create both, better and worse results, which is why further investigation in this regard is needed.

4   FlexMash 2.0 – Level of Maturity

The FlexMash tool, although being a research project developed by a small group supported by student thesis', has reached a high level of maturity throughout its 2 year long development. The first stable version of FlexMash was presented during the ICWE Rapid Mashup Challenge 2015 in Rotterdam, the second version, which is described in this article, was presented in the 2016 edition of this challenge in Lugano. The FlexMash implementation is provided as an open source project on GitHub[1] and is licensed under the Apache 2.0 license. We hope to increase the community of developers to even increase the level of maturity in the future.

However, although the maturity of FlexMash could have been increased with the latest features, there are still some issues and many features that are planned for the future. For example, enhanced interactivity, an extended set of data sources and data operations, the support of further non-functional requirements, and, as a consequence further execution components.

5   FlexMash 2.0 – Feature Checklist

In this section, the features of the current state of FlexMash's implementation are described based on the ICWE Rapid Mashup Challenge checklist, which contains

---

[1] https://github.com/hirmerpl/FlexMash.

information about important properties and design choices of mashup tools to enable their categorization. The feature checklist is based on related work and is subdivided into two parts: (i) an overall *mashup feature checklist* as described in [5] (Chap. 6), and (ii) *a mashup tool feature checklist* as described in [1]. The detailed information about the single entries are provided in these references.

- Mashup Feature Checklist
  - **Mashup Type:** Data mashups
  - **Component Type:** Data components
  - **Runtime Location:** Both client and server
  - **Integration Logic:** Orchestrated integration
  - **Instantiation Lifecycle:** Stateless
- Mashup Tool Feature Checklist
  - **Targeted End-User:** Non programmers
  - **Automation Degree:** Semi-automation
  - **Liveness Level:** Level 3 – Automatic compilation and deployment, requires re-initialization
  - **Interaction Technique:** Visual language (Iconic)
  - **Online User Community:** None (yet)

6   ICWE Rapid Mashup Challenge

This section describes all aspects of the Rapid Mashup Challenge (RMC) 2016 in Lugano, ranging from the scenario we presented, the demo flow, the preparations for this challenge, and discussions and findings we collected.

6.1   Scenario and Demo Flow

This section introduces the scenario we presented during the Rapid Mashup Challenge 2016, which focuses on data integration and analytics. This scenario analyzes if weather conditions influence the amount and types of traffic accidents. Basis for the analyses are the New York City Police Department Motor Vehicle Collisions[2] data set and a data set extracted from the Open Weather API[3]. Consequently, we focus our analyses on New York City exclusively, however, due to the generic nature of the analysis, further data sets are also easy applicable.

The NYPD Motor Vehicle Collisions data set contains all documented accidents from 2012 until today. Currently there are 800,000 entries in the data set. Each entry contains the following information: (i) date and time of the accident, (ii) location information containing street name, zip code, borough as well as latitude and longitude, (iii) whether and how many persons (separated in drivers, cyclists, motorists, pedestrians) have been injured or killed, (iv) the cause for the accident (if known), and (v) the amount and types of vehicles (e.g., bus, taxi,

---

[2] https://data.cityofnewyork.us/Public-Safety/NYPD-Motor-Vehicle-Collisions/h9gi-nx95.

[3] http://openweathermap.org/api.

FlexMash Builder

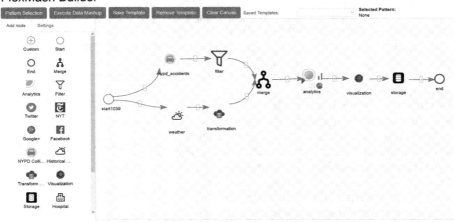

Fig. 9. Mashup Plan to run the analyses of the scenario shown at the RMC

bicycle, passenger vehicle, and many more) involved. The data from the Open Weather API for New York City provides the following information: (i) date, (ii) temperature, (iii) amount of precipitation, (iv) amount of snowfall, and (v) wind speed. In our scenario, we analyze the following questions based on the given data:

1. Does the temperature influence the amount of occurring accidents?
2. Does the precipitation influence the amount of occurring accidents?
3. Does the wind speed influence the amount of occurring accidents?
4. Are certain vehicle types influenced more by weather conditions (e.g., buses)?

To run these analyses, we use our data mashup tool FlexMash. The basis for this is the Pipes and Filters based Mashup Plan depicted in Fig. 9. To model these analyses, we have to create the depicted model step by step using the Flex-Mash modeling tool. First, a start node is inserted into the canvas. Start nodes mainly serve overview purposes and are not a necessary means to model these Mashup Plan. The entry points can also be determined automatically through topological sorting. Second, we insert the data sources, i.e., the NYPD Motor Vehicle Collisions data set provided through a REST interface, and the Open Weather Data provided by a CSV file. The data sources are abstracted through two Data Source Descriptions that extract the data as a whole from these two data sets. These Data Source Descriptions are also inserted into the canvas and are connected to the start node. Third, the NYPD accidents DSD is connected to a filter node (DPD), which is necessary to realize the fourth analysis, which investigates different types of vehicles. Through the settings of this filter node, the type of vehicle can be chosen accordingly. Furthermore, we connect the weather data DPD to a transformation node, which can be configured to transform the temperature provided in Fahrenheit to Celcius. These nodes are inserted and

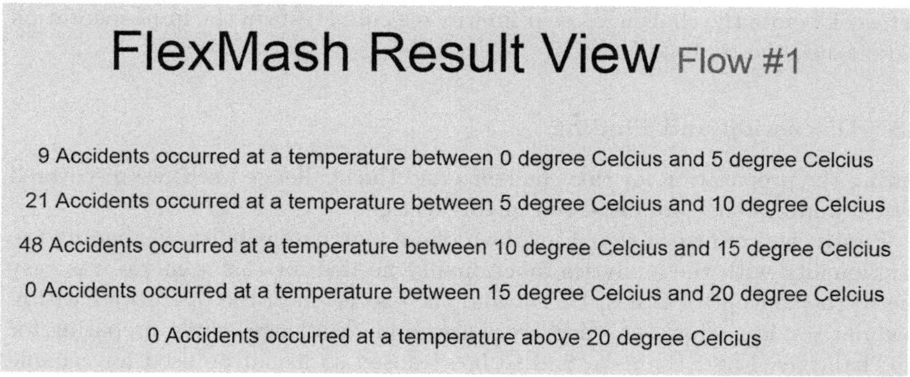

FlexMash Result View Flow #1

9 Accidents occurred at a temperature between 0 degree Celcius and 5 degree Celcius

21 Accidents occurred at a temperature between 5 degree Celcius and 10 degree Celcius

48 Accidents occurred at a temperature between 10 degree Celcius and 15 degree Celcius

0 Accidents occurred at a temperature between 15 degree Celcius and 20 degree Celcius

0 Accidents occurred at a temperature above 20 degree Celcius

Fig. 10. Analytics result of the FlexMash tool shown at the RMC

connected as depicted in Fig. 9. Next, the data is merged to receive a common data set. The merging of the data is done in a straight-forward manner by a join over the date and time columns. This can be done easily because there is no overlap in the data, and therefore there are no conflicts possible. Furthermore, the data of these columns are structured in a similar manner. To model this merge operation, we insert a merge node DPD into the canvas and connect it accordingly. Based on the merged data, we conduct a simple analysis that groups the accidents according to the weather conditions. Which weather condition is used for grouping, e.g. temperature or wind speed, can be chosen in the settings of the analytics node. After that, we connect the analytics node to a visualization node that depicts the analytics results as HTML (cf., Fig. 10). This HTML text is then stored in a file by connecting it to the storage node. This node can be configured in different ways: data can be stored in files or in different databases. Based on this model, the four different analyses can be executed only by slightly adjusting the settings of the nodes. This especially shows the ad-hoc capabilities of FlexMash and, furthermore, that an explorative behavior is possible due to an easy adaptation and re-execution of the model.

6.2   Challenge Preparations

We had four weeks to prepare for this challenge. To do so, we had to conduct several preparations regarding the FlexMash tool and the presented scenario. First, we did a refactoring of FlexMash's code to enable a more modular, loosely coupled application, which is easier to extend. Next, we provided DSDs and DPDs for the scenarios and we implemented corresponding services that realize the data processing operations. Because of the high extensibility of FlexMash, the preparations did not take a lot of time. Due to the limited complexity of the scenario, three weeks of implementation were sufficient. The implementation of the interactive node has been finished prior to the challenge preparations. In the last week before the challenge, we primarily executed tests of the implementation and cleaned the code.

6.3   Discussion and Findings

During the preparation for this challenge and the challenge itself, we discovered several findings that are discussed in this section.

Firstly, we confirmed that FlexMash offers high extensibility. Extending the functionality with the analytics functionality needed for this scenario was easy due to the concept of DSDs, DPDs, and the execution of the operations within modular services. However, there were also some challenges while preparing for the challenge. First, the data had to be cleansed so it can be used for reliable analysis, i.e., errors, missing fields etc. had to be deleted first, which was a cumbersome task. Second, it was hard to find the weather data for the location at the specific time range due to the fact that a lot of weather APIs only provide the data for a payment. As a consequence, we did not find weather data for the whole time range of the accident data. Because of that, we could only analyze a subset of the data.

There are still some limitations regarding the implemented scenario although it only serves demonstration purposes: the analyses are implemented in a straight-forward manner, i.e., we only count the occurrences of accidents for a specific range of temperature, precipitation, and so on. Furthermore, the nodes are not very generic, that is, they currently only work for this specific scenario. In the future, we will provide more generic nodes for data extraction and for analytics.

7   Related Work

This section introduces related work and describes a detailed separation of Flex-Mash with other approaches that have the same goal – efficient processing and integration of heterogeneous data. These are approved ETL (Extract Transform Load) tools such as Pentaho[4], data analytics tools such as KNIME[5] or RapidMiner[6] and information integration tools such as informatica[7]. We use the following criteria to compare the FlexMash approach with related work:

- **Extensibility.** We define an approach as fully *extensible*, if it provides a means to extend the set of supported data sources and data operations.
- **Cloud support.** We define an approach as fully *cloud supported*, if it provides a means to execute the data processing in a virtual cloud environment. More precisely, it has to support automated provisioning, distribution of load, scalability, and availability.

---

[4] http://www.pentaho.com/.
[5] https://www.knime.org/.
[6] https://rapidminer.com/.
[7] https://www.informatica.com.

Criteria \ Approach	ETL Tools	Data Analytics Tools	Information Integration Tools	FlexMash
Extensibility	Medium Support	Low Support	Low Support	High Support
Cloud support	High Support	Full Support	Full Support	Full Support
Graphical modeling / Usability	High Support	Low Support	Low Support	High Support
Flexible execution	Medium Support	Medium Support	Medium Support	Full Support
User interaction during runtime	No Support	Low Support	No Support	Medium Support

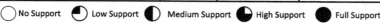

◯ No Support   ◔ Low Support   ◑ Medium Support   ◕ High Support   ● Full Support

Fig. 11. Classification of the FlexMash approach

- **Usability.** We define an approach as fully *usable*, if it provides an easy modeling of data integration and processing scenarios, preferably graphically and support for users outside the IT area, i.e., users without extensive programming expertise.
- **Flexibility.** We define an approach as fully *flexible*, if it provides adaptations tailor-made for the specific user. For example, by providing a configurable execution and not a fixed, static one.
- **User interactivity during runtime.** We define an approach as fully *interactive*, if the user has the possibility to monitor and control the execution during modeling and during runtime.

For each approach or tool related to FlexMash, we will provide examples to be able to provide a fair comparison (Fig. 11).

7.1 Extensibility

We compared the extensibility of different approaches and we found out, that ETL tools and information integration tools offer a good extensibility. For example, new data sources can be added easily to these platforms to be integrated and processed. However, in regard to the extension of data processing operations in the sense that new algorithms or self-made data operations can be added is not supported by most platforms. More precisely, the concept of *bring your own code* is oftentimes not supported. In contrast, data analytics tools such as Knime and RapidMiner support the extension with new data operations, e.g., new analytics algorithms. These can, for example, be added using the programming language *R*. However, the extension with new data sources on the other hand is not fully supported. As a consequence, related approaches are only extensible to a certain degree, either enabling the integration of new data sources or data operations but not both. Because of that, we classify these approaches as medium extensible.

FlexMash offers a high degree of extensibility through its generic approach. By enabling an easy adding of services to extract data from various data sources and processing data, FlexMash enables bringing own code into the system. However, a fully generic approach also increases the complexity of the extension of new data sources and operations. As a consequence, we classify FlexMash as highly extensible. In the future, we will provide an easy-to-use interface to extend the set of data sources and data operations.

7.2 Cloud Support

When examining the related approaches, we found out that most of them offer great support of virtualized cloud environments, even providing a means for automated distribution of load and scaling of virtual machines. Especially the platforms Pentaho, informatica, and the IBM analytics services of their cloud platform Bluemix cope with the cloud-based processing of data very efficiently. FlexMash also supports cloud-based execution as well as the distribution of load on different scalable virtual machines as described in Sect. 3.2. Consequently, we classify all approaches as fully cloud supported.

7.3 Usability

Due to the fact that usability cannot be easily measured and requires extensive user studies, we only focus on the aspect whether in our opinion users have to have knowledge about programming and algorithms or if domain users such as business experts can use these tools. Information integration tools focus on the usability by non-programmers, i.e., by domain-experts in enterprises. Due to this fact, the technical details are well hidden from the users so we can classify information integration tools as fully usable. ETL tools and data analytics tools in contrast expect a lot of specific knowledge from their users. Although the source code is mostly hidden from the user, extensive, detailed parameterization has to be provided on the modeling level. This parameterization, however, can only be provided if the algorithms, data sources and data operations are fully understood. Because of that, in our opinion, we classify these tools as lowly usable (for domain-experts). FlexMash offers a full abstraction from technical details by the introduced Mashup Plans that are transformed into executable representations. The parameterization is kept simple and in a way that domain-experts can understand. Furthermore, FlexMash provides means for visual interaction during runtime (cf. Sect. 3.3). As a consequence, FlexMash can be classified as fully usable.

7.4 Flexibility

In our examination of the different tools, we found out that there is a huge gap regarding the flexibility of the execution. More precisely, all available tools only offer one way to execute the integration and processing of data. However, the execution should depend on the use case scenario, and the requirements of the tool's users. Although some tools offer a means to configure the execution, there is no support for a tailor-made execution specific to the users' needs. FlexMash enables this flexibility by enabling a tailor-made execution of data integration and processing based on non-functional requirements as described in Sect. 3. Therefore, we classify FlexMash as fully flexible.

7.5 Interactivity

Another gap we discovered in the approaches we examined was the interactivity during modeling and execution. Especially interaction during runtime is not supported at all. We close this gap by introducing an approach to extend FlexMash with interactivity during runtime (cf., Sect. 3.3) so that users can easily monitor and control the execution, which is expected to lead to improved results. This will be especially addressed in our future work.

7.6 Conclusion

We found out that although there are many tools that have the same goal as FlexMash, they cannot fulfill all criteria that are in our opinion important. Flex-Mash can cope with most of these criteria and therefore provides a comprehensive solution. We are aware that commercial products can provide a wider selection of data sources and data operations as well as a more efficient processing through several years of code optimizations. However, we discovered several gaps they cannot cope with. FlexMash mainly serves as proof of concept that these gaps can be closed.

8   Summary and Outlook

In this article, we presented the data mashup tool FlexMash, more precisely, the second version of FlexMash that was presented during the ICWE Rapid Mashup Challenge 2016. FlexMash is a tool that enables flexible execution of data mashups based on the user's non-functional requirements. Furthermore, FlexMash offers domain-specific modeling based on the Pipes and Filters pattern that enables usage by domain-experts, even without extensive programming knowledge. As mentioned in the introduction, FlexMash can serve as a way to deal with the Big Data problem, which is defined through *the three Vs*: *Variety*, *Velocity* and *Volume*. As thoroughly explained throughout this paper, our approach can handle the Variety issue quite well. The Volume issue can also be handled through the high scalability of the approach enabled by cloud-based execution. Each data processing operation can be conducted in different virtual machines that can be scaled independently. Consequently, large data sets can be handled. However, we found out that some execution engines, especially those based on BPEL, cannot cope with transferring large data sets from one service to another. To cope with this issue, we provide caches to store intermediate data. Based on this, only the key to the corresponding entry in the cache is handed from one service to another to cope with the issues of some engines handing over large data sets. The Velocity issue, meaning that data changes frequently, can be partially handled by FlexMash. Once data changes, the Mashup Plan has to be re-transformed and re-deployed to involve the new data. However, with data sets that change very often, this leads to efficiency issues. Currently, we are working on a solution for that by computing intermediate results during modeling time so the whole Mashup Plan does not have to be re-transformed and re-executed. In addition to the original definition, a wide variety of other V's are existing, most commonly *Veracity* and *Value* whose support by FlexMash is hereinafter described. Our approach to bring in the user into the process allows a deeper and more detailed understanding of the data characteristic and content. For this reason, we can expect the user to be aware of the data quality as well as data trustworthiness, i.e., we fulfill Veracity. In respect to the last V, Value, our approach offers more control, steering the analysis process based on the objective of the domain expert and, as a consequence, more satisfying and more accurate results.

For the challenge, we showed the capabilities of FlexMash using a scenario that examines whether traffic accidents correlate with weather conditions. By doing so, we examined the conditions precipitation, snowfall, and temperature. Additionally, we showed how FlexMash can be enhanced with interactivity during runtime. We further described the preparation for this challenge and which findings we could discover by participating. For future work, we will focus on the interaction during mashup runtime because this is an interesting concept and can highly improve the usability. Furthermore, we are working on a new and improved user interface. Our goal is presenting these results during the next Rapid Mashup Challenge 2017.

References

1. Aghaee, S., Nowak, M., Pautasso, C.: Reusable 'decision space for mashup tool design. In: 4th ACM SIGCHI Symposium on Engineering Interactive Computing Systems (EICS 2012), Copenhagen, Denmark, pp. 211–220, June 2012
2. Binz, T., Breitenbücher, U., Kopp, O., Leymann, F.: TOSCA: portable automated deployment and management of cloud applications. In: Bouguettaya, A., Sheng, Q.Z., Daniel, F. (eds.) Advanced Web Services, pp. 527–549. Springer, New York, Januar 2014. http://www2.informatik.uni-stuttgart.de/cgi-bin/NCSTRL/NCSTRL_view.pl?id=INBOOK-2014-01&engl=0
3. Binz, T., Breitenbücher, U., Haupt, F., Kopp, O., Leymann, F., Nowak, A., Wagner, S.: OpenTOSCA – a runtime for TOSCA-based cloud applications. In: Basu, S., Pautasso, C., Zhang, L., Fu, X. (eds.) ICSOC 2013. LNCS, vol. 8274, pp. 692–695. Springer, Heidelberg (2013). doi:10.1007/978-3-642-45005-1_62
4. Breitenbücher, U., Binz, T., Képes, K., Kopp, O., Leymann, F., Wettinger, J.: Combining declarative and imperative cloud application provisioning based on TOSCA. In: Proceedings of the IEEE International Conference on Cloud Engineering (IC2E), pp. 87–96. IEEE Computer Society, März 2014. http://www2.informatik.uni-stuttgart.de/cgi-bin/NCSTRL/NCSTRL_view.pl?id=INPROC-2014-21&engl=0

5. Daniel, F., Matera, M.: Mashups - Concepts Models and Architectures. Data-Centric Systems and Applications. Springer, Heidelberg (2014)
6. Hirmer, P., Breitenbücher, U., Binz, T., Leymann, F.: Automatic topology completion of TOSCA-based cloud applications. In: Proceedings des CloudCycle14 Workshops auf der 44. Jahrestagung der Gesellschaft für Informatik e.V. (GI). LNI, vol. 232, pp. 247–258. Gesellschaft für Informatik e.V. (GI), Bonn. http://www2.informatik.uni-stuttgart.de/cgi-bin/NCSTRL/NCSTRL_view.pl?id=INPROC-2014-66&engl=0
7. Hirmer, P., Breitenbücher, U., Binz, T., Leymann, F.: FlexMash – flexible data mashups based on pattern-based model transformation. In: Daniel, F., Pautasso, C. (eds.) Rapid Mashup Development Tools. CCIS, vol. 591, pp. 12–30. Springer, Cham (2016). doi:10.1007/978-3-319-28727-0_2.
8. Hirmer, P., Mitschang, B.: TOSCA4Mashups - enhanced method for on-demand data mashup provisioning. In: Proceedings of the 10th Symposium and Summer School on Service-Oriented Computing (2016)
9. Hirmer, P., Reimann, P., Wieland, M., Mitschang, B.: Extended techniques for flexible modeling and execution of data mashups. In: Proceedings of the 4th International Conference on Data Management Technologies and Applications (DATA), April 2015
10. Kandel, S., Heer, J., Plaisant, C., Kennedy, J., van Ham, F., Riche, N.H., Weaver, C., Lee, B., Brodbeck, D., Buono, P.: Research directions in data wrangling: visualizations and transformations for usable and credible data. Inform. Vis. $10(4)$, 271–288. http://ivi.sagepub.com/lookup/doi/10.1177/1473871611415994
11. Kemper, H.G., Baars, H., Mehanna, W.: Business Intelligence - Grundlagen und praktische Anwendungen. Vieweg+Teubner, Wiesbaden (2010). http://link.springer.com/10.1007/978-3-8348-9727-5
12. Kopp, O., Binz, T., Breitenbücher, U., Leymann, F.: Winery – a modeling tool for TOSCA-based cloud applications. In: Basu, S., Pautasso, C., Zhang, L., Fu, X. (eds.) ICSOC 2013. LNCS, vol. 8274, pp. 700–704. Springer, Heidelberg (2013). doi:10.1007/978-3-642-45005-1_64
13. Meunier, R.: The pipes and filters architecture. In: Pattern languages of program design (1995)
14. OASIS: Topology and Orchestration Specification for Cloud Applications (2013)
15. OASIS: TOSCA Primer. http://docs.oasis-open.org/tosca/tosca-primer/v1.0/cnd01/tosca-primer-v1.0-cnd01.pdf
16. Savikhin, A., Maciejewski, R., Ebert, D.S.: Applied Visual Analytics for Economic Decision-Making (2008)
17. Shneiderman, B.: Inventing discovery tools: combining information visualization with data mining. Inform. Vis. $1(1)$, 5–12 (2002). http://ivi.sagepub.com/content/1/1/5.abstract
18. Wang, X., Jeong, D.H., Dou, W., Lee, S.W., Ribarsky, W., Chang, R.: Defining and applying knowledge conversion processes to a visual analytics system. Comput. Graph. $33(5)$, 616–623 (2009)

The SmartComposition Approach for Creating Environment-Aware Multi-screen Mashups

Michael Krug$^{(\boxtimes)}$, Fabian Wiedemann, Markus Ast, and Martin Gaedke

Technische Universität Chemnitz, Chemnitz, Germany
{michael.krug,fabian.wiedemann,markus.ast,
martin.gaedke}@informatik.tu-chemnitz.de

Abstract. Mashups aim to enable non-experts to compose complex applications by combining various existing building blocks. The special case of user interface mashups is focusing on the composition of user interface components. In this paper, we present our SmartComposition approach as an UI mashup framework that supports local developers in creating environment-aware multi-screen mashups. We aim for simplicity and focus on the definition of mashup scenarios by only using HTML markup. Therefore, we facilitate Web Component technologies to build SmartComponents – the building blocks in our approach. For achieving environment-awareness, our approach integrates features of the Web of Things into mashups, such as controlling actors and accessing sensors. SmartComposition provides mashup composition by external communication configuration through markup. We additionally propose the distribution of mashup components and their communication across multiple screens using a messaging service utilizing WebSockets.

Keywords: Mashup · User-interface mashup · Multi-screen mashup · Web Components · HTML5 · Web of Things

1 Introduction

Mashups aim at enabling non-experts to create rich web applications [1]. Daniel and Matera define the term *mashup* as: "a composite application developed starting from reusable data, application logic, and/or user interfaces typically, but not mandatorily, sourced from the Web" [2]. The amount of tools for creating such mashups significantly increased within the last years. In this paper, we focus on the special case of user interface mashups that particularly deal with the composition of user interface components. While other approaches focus on automatic or semi-automatic mashup creation and deployment to desktop as well as mobile screens, our approach eases the creation of UI mashups that run distributed across several screens, so called multi-screen mashups.

"The Web of Things is a specialization of the Internet of Things that uses what made the web so successful and applies it to embedded devices in order to make the latest developments in the Internet of Things accessible to as many

© Springer International Publishing AG 2017
F. Daniel and M. Gaedke (Eds.): RMC 2016, CCIS 696, pp. 30–50, 2017.
DOI: 10.1007/978-3-319-53174-8_3

developers as possible." [5] Thus, the Web of Things (WoT) describes approaches and patterns to connect real-word objects to the World Wide Web by reusing existing Web standards [6]. WoT offers the possibility of controlling devices in the physical world or even accessing remote sensor data [8]. In this domain two main concepts exist: actors and sensors. While actors are defined by doing something physical, such as producing something, sensors are defined by observing the physical world for example, measures like temperature.

The purpose of SmartComposition is to enable local developers to create multi-screen mashups with environmental awareness. Our approach is based on basic web technologies, such as HTML5 and CSS. Thus, a local developer who is familiar with these technologies does not require advanced knowledge of JavaScript or programming in general. For achieving a high level of reuse our approach requires loosely coupling and a suitable communication infrastructure to minimize the overhead when integrating them. While common mashup platforms require deploying and hosting their components in a separate runtime environments, we want to eliminate this requirement and enable usage in any standard HTML5 website or application.

With the emerging field and availability of WoT entities, there is an increase in potential applications of end-user-based composition of functionality. Implementing WoT entities as components, integrating them into mashups and applying inter-component communication to them, yields a huge amount of new possible use cases and eases end-users to compose WoT entities on their own. That is, we want to show how WoT entities can composed using our SmartComposition approach.

The rest of this paper is organized as follows: In Sect. 2, we state two exemplary scenarios to motivate the concept of mashups. Following, in Sect. 3, we present the SmartComposition approach and outline relevant aspects and components. Section 4 gives a detailed insight of the presented mashup, the preparation and the flow of the live demonstration. Finally, we conclude our paper and provide the requested feature checklist in Sect. 7.

2   Scenarios

We want to show how mashups can be used by describing two exemplary scenarios. The first scenario is based on the media enrichment concept described in [10]. The central point of this use case is a media fragment – more precisely a video. This video deals with a specific topic, shows different places, people and other things. While normally a user would need to search for more information about the shown content himself, media enrichment aims to provide the user directly with related information without the need of initializing the search on his own (cf. Fig. 1). Thus, there are a lot of ways and information sources to enrich this media consumption scenario. The most prominent ones are, for example, the visualization of geographical places on a map, images from a place or person shown or mentioned in the video, textual background information from an encyclopedia, a list of related videos, posts from social networks about the

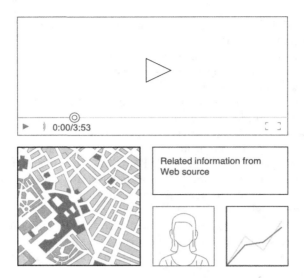

Fig. 1. Example media enrichment scenario with a video and other components

Fig. 2. Example dashboard (http://themifycloud.com/demos/templates/joli/)

topic and many more. Those information artifacts can be provided as user interface components. The challenge is to solve the composition and deployment of
those components to create an "integrative" application. The application of the
mashup concept offers a good solution for this enrichment scenario.

A second scenario we like to discuss is a control panel or dashboard application as shown in Fig. 2. In management information systems, a dashboard is

user interface, showing a graphical presentation of various statuses or trends to improve decision making. Thus, it consists of multiple single information representation blocks that visualize data. In addition to this, control components to modify parameters of remote or local services or components can exist. For example, a user could select a location or date for which the data is curated.

We could think of multiple data source components that provide the dashboard with the information needed, multiple user interface components that are capable of visualizing different types of data as well as control elements like sliders or selections to influence the visualizations. By the composition of such standalone building blocks, this scenario could be realized.

In the next section, we present our SmartComposition approach, whose goal is to ease the creation of various mashup scenarios including the described ones.

3   The SmartComposition Approach

SmartComposition describes how to define independent, encapsulated, configurable and loosely coupled components using standard web technologies as well as their composition to create single- and multi-screen mashups. We focus on simplicity and emphasize the creation of mashups by only using HTML markup without the requirement of a dedicated runtime environment. This lowers the barrier for local developers to create complex applications by composition of multiple components. As displayed in Fig. 3, the SmartComposition approach consists of the following components, which will be described in more detail later:

SmartComponents. The building-blocks of our approach are called Smart-Components. Other approaches often used the term *widget* to describe those

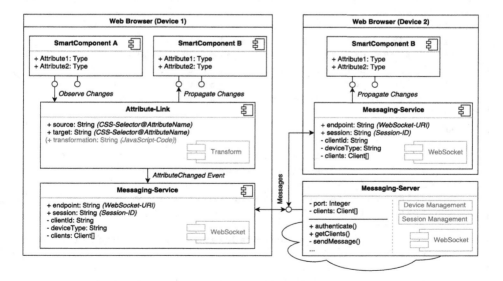

Fig. 3. Components and overview of the SmartComposition approach

kinds of components. Since our components do not necessarily need to have a user interface part, we decided to not call them widgets.

Attribute-Link. To compose SmartComponents and enable information exchange, we provide an Attribute-Link component that is capable of connecting two attribute endpoints. The configuration is done in markup and also supports data transformation.

Messaging-Service. The Messaging-Service is the client-side counterpart of the Messaging-Server that enables the distribution of communication events across multiple devices. It integrates seamlessly with the existing mashup and does not need any altering of the SmartComponents to provide message distribution.

Messaging-Server. On the server side, a Messaging-Server handles the selective message distribution as well as the management of connected devices and separated sessions. The bidirectional, low-latency communication channel is implemented using the WebSocket protocol.

Listing 1 shows an example of how a SmartComposition mashup defined in markup will look like. It represents a scenario where a user can enter a location into an input box that will be shown on a map by geocoding the string value into geographic coordinates using three connected components. The example states the component instances for a basic HTML input element, a Google-Geocoder and a Google-Map as well as the inter-component communication configuration using a Messaging-Service and multiple Attribute-Link elements. The Messaging-Service in this example is optional, since there is no need for any distribution. All necessary dependencies and component definition files are imported at the top in the *head* section.

```
<html lang="en">
<head>
  <link rel="import"href="polymer.html">
  <link rel="import"href="SmartComponent.html">
  <link rel="import"href="AttributeLink.html">
  <link rel="import"href="MessagingService.html">
  <link rel="import"href="components.html">
</head>
<body>
  <input type="text"
         onchange="this.setAttribute('value', this.value)">
  <google-geocoder></google-geocoder>
  <google-map></google-map>
  <messaging-service endpoint="endpoint:port">
    <attribute-link
        source="input@value"
        target="google-geocoder@address"></attribute-link>
    <attribute-link
        source="google-geocoder@lat"
        target="google-map@lat"></attribute-link>
    <attribute-link
```

```
         source ="google - geocoder@lng"
         target ="google - map@lng "></attribute - link >
   </messaging - service >
</body >
</html >
```

Listing 1. Simple SmartComposition mashup example in HTML markup

To achieve our goal of simplicity and re-usability, SmartCompositionleverages a set of new W3C specifications called *Web Components* for defining and implementing *SmartComponents*. Web Components are based on the following specifications: *Templates* [12], *Custom Elements* [14], *HTML Imports* [15] and *Shadow DOM* [16]. SmartComponents can form user interface, data or logic components as well as a combination of those types. They can be used in any HTML5-based web application and do not require a dedicated runtime environment or portal software to be executed. Our components are independent, encapsulated, configurable and programmable. Following, we present these characteristics in more detail.

Independency. For the execution or presentation of SmartComponents no runtime environment other than a browser is needed. In contrast to Packaged Web Apps (W3C widgets), where a server application like Apache Wookie is required, we enable the usage in any HTML5-based web application.

Encapsulation. SmartComponents do not interfere with other elements of the web application. By using technologies like Shadow DOM or Local Dom each component has its own scope, where for example, its style definitions are valid. Thus, a developer does not need to take care of conflict free IDs or CSS statements when creating new components.

Configurability. By exploiting the already available interfaces of HTML elements – their attributes – SmartComponents can be configured within the markup. There is no need of calling complex scripts for the initial set up of a component.

Programmability. Since SmartComponents are registered as stateful DOM elements and also work like standard DOM elements, they can be instantiated in markup or programmatically, respond to property and attribute changes and provide methods to manipulate their internal state. Developers are also able to influence the behavior of the running components with standard DOM methods.

To ease the development of new SmartComponents, we are using *Polymer*[1] as an underlying framework. Polymer offers a comprehensive implementation of the Web Components standards. It provides a declarative syntax to define new components and supports for example, event & data binding and advanced template features. Furthermore, by including *webcomponents.js*[2] we also enables the usage of those technologies in older browsers that do not support them natively.

---

[1] https://www.polymer-project.org/1.0/.

[2] https://github.com/webcomponents/webcomponentsjs.

Additionally, we integrate user interaction features like moving SmartComponents by drag-and-drop as well as the option to migrate components to other connected screens with their state preserved. SmartComponents can be added, removed and reconfigured at any time either by their user interface controls or programmatically. To give an insight of the structure and the creation process of a SmartComponent, we will go into detail of a single *example-component* in the following subsection.

3.1   Structure of SmartComponents

To build a *SmartComponent*, a developer needs to prepare at least one file that consists of three parts: the definition of the template, the styling and the logic (see Fig. 4). All this code is stored within an HTML-file. As it is displayed in listing 2, all parts are defined within markup. This structure is given by the Polymer framework that we use as the basis for creating SmartComponents. All code is encapsulated in a tag called *dom-module* that has a unique id attribute assigned. In this tag the *template* and the *script* tag is embedded. The *template* contains all static HTML content of the component as well as possible data binding references. Besides that, the style definition is included that is scoped only to the new component. The developer can use standard CSS statements to customize the look of the SmartComponent. Since SmartComponents offer encapsulation, those style definitions do not conflict with other components in the same web application.

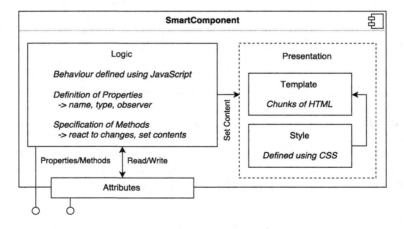

Fig. 4. Internal structure of a SmartComponent

```
<dom-module id="example-component">
  <template>
    <style>
    <!-- CSS definition statements -->
    </style>
```

```
    <!-- Static HTML code with possible data bindings -->
  </template>
  <script>
    <!-- JS code for definition of the components logic -->
  </script>
</dom-module>
```

Listing 2. Parts of a SmartComponent Definition File

Listing 3 shows an exemplary template definition. Within the *style* tag the actual component element can be referred to with the *:host* pseudo-class. Polymer supports several options to make the HTML template more dynamic in terms of data bindings. For example, one can iterate over an array containing multiple elements by using the *template is="dom-repeat"* statement. Now all the content specified in this statement is repeatedly placed in the components DOM and filled with the actual content of the elements. By using double curly braces the properties of the elements can be accessed and their value is automatically placed at the stated position. Furthermore, this template statement is dynamically updated when the referenced JavaScript object is changed.

The actual behavior of the SmartComponent is defined within the *script* tag and follows a declarative syntax. As displayed in listing 4, the declaration is stated using the *Polymer* function. The developer has to state a unique name that needs to contain a dash and should refer to the id attribute of the parent *dom-module* tag. Additionally, the properties of the component can be declared by stating their name, type, initial value and other options. To observe changed values of properties to, for example, call a function, one can either state an observer function directly in the property declaration or in the separate *observers* array. In the *observers* array a function name and all the properties that shall be observed are specified. Furthermore, all functions the component needs to work as desired are declared. For example, setting properties that are then rendered to the visible user interface, making API calls, etc.

```
<template>
  <style>
    :host { display: inline-block; }
    #container { width: 100
  </style>
  <div id="container">
  <template is="dom-repeat"items="{{output}}"as="item">
    <p><b>{{item.name}}</b><span>{{item.value}}</span></p>
  </template>
  </div>
</template>
```

Listing 3. Style and content definition within the declaration file

```
<script>
  Polymer({
    is:"example-component",
    properties: {
      count: {
        type: Number, value: 4, reflectToAttribute: true
      },
      language: {
        type: String, value:"en", reflectToAttribute: true,
        observer:"someFunction"
      },
      output: {
        type: Array, reflectToAttribute: true
      }
    },
    observers: [
     "propertiesChanged(count, language)"
    ],
    propertiesChanged: function() {
      this.someFunction();
    },
    someFunction: function() {
      //do something with this.count and this.language
      this.output = [ { name:"Test", value:"Example"} ];
    }
  });
</script>
```

Listing 4. Definition of the SmartComponent's properties and function

One option that can be stated for each property and we need to especially highlight is *reflectToAttribute: true*. This setting enables SmartComponents to provide their interfaces as attributes in the markup, which enables the composition through configuration as described later in Subsect. 3.2. Thus, any change of the property is reflected to its according attribute and the other way around. By exploiting this feature, the developer is not required to handle the propagation of values to the attributes by himself. Following, we introduce our inter-component communication solution.

3.2   Inter-Component Communication

In contrast to our contribution [11] to last year's "Rapid Mashup Challenge", we shift from including communication aspects inside the components to an external composition solution while still focusing on loosely coupling. This enables a better control of the information flow inside the mashup. To achieve this, we design SmartComponents as DOM-Elements that provide their in- and output interfaces through attributes accordingly. We enable mashup composition by linking those attributes through external configuration.

We connect the attribute interfaces of SmartComponents using a stand-alone *Attribute-Link* component, which is configured by a *source* and *target* selector and an optional *transformation* function. The *Attribute-Link* component is also implemented as a SmartComponent and can be deployed directly in the markup without knowledge of JavaScript. To address a component within the mashup, we use the established *CSS selector* syntax[3]. This syntax is applied to both the source as well as the target selector. Since CSS selectors can return multiple elements, we also support multiple components as target and source. The attribute is addressed by its name separated by an @ sign. Example: `geo-coder#id1@address`. To define complex inter-component communication setups, the *Attribute-Link* can be included multiple times in an applications. We use native *DOM mutation observers*[4] to watch for attribute changes without affecting the responsiveness of the application. Additionally, we support data transformation by offering to specify a transformation function within the *Attribute-Link* configuration. If such a function was specified, it will be applied and the resulting value is then propagated to the defined attribute of the according target component. Up next, the extension of the local communication to a distributed one is presented.

```
<attribute-link source="selector@attribute"
                target="selector@attribute">
                transformation="JavaScript-Code"/*Optional*/>
</attribute-link>
```

Listing 5. Markup syntax of the Attribute-Link component

3.3   Inter-Device Communication

In our approach, we also focus on the creation of distributed or multi-screen mashups. Thus, we additionally enable the addressing of target components on multiple *connected devices* (browsers running the mashup application with the same endpoint configured that share the same context). We achieve this by proposing a *Messaging-Service* component and a *Messaging-Server*. The *Messaging-Server* is implemented using Node.js[5] and uses the *WebSocket protocol*[6] that provides a bi-directional, low-latency communication channel. As displayed in Fig. 6, the *Messaging-Server* also takes care of the device and session management. This includes authentication, grouping of connected devices for selective message distribution and the transmission of the device and client information to all participants.

We propose the *Messaging-Service* to follow the same principles as all our components. Thus, it is also implemented as a SmartComponent and therefore

---

[3] Selectors Level 3 https://www.w3.org/TR/selectors/.

[4] DOM Standard https://dom.spec.whatwg.org/#mutation-observers.

[5] Node.js https://nodejs.org/.

[6] The WebSocket Protocol http://tools.ietf.org/html/rfc6455.

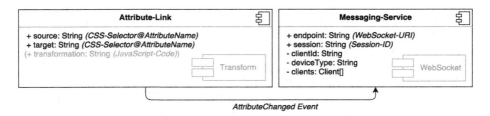

Fig. 5. Attribute-Link propagating changed attributes to a Messaging-Service

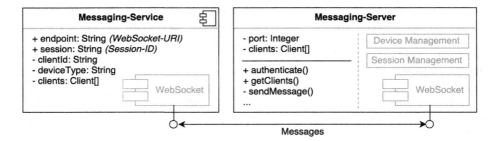

Fig. 6. Messaging-Service and Messaging-Server communicating using WebSockets

can be instantiated and configured in the same way by just using markup. The *Attribute-Link* component seamlessly integrates with the *Messaging-Service* by placing it in the DOM as a child element like display in listing 6. Changed attributes that shall be distributed are signaled by dispatching a custom event (see Fig. 5). This event contains the target component selector, the attribute name and the new value.

The *Messaging-Service* contacts the *Messaging-Server*, which then distributes the message to other *connected devices* (cf. Fig. 3). The propagation of the received messages to the target components on the remote devices running the mashup requires an instance of an accordingly configured *Messaging-Service* component. To only target remote components, we also provide a configuration option called "no-local-link".

```
<messaging-service endpoint="protocol://address:port"
                   session="Session-Identifier">
       <attribute-link source target [...]></attribute-link>
</messaging-service>
```

Listing 6. Syntax of the Messaging-Service in combination with an Attribute-Link

3.4   Integrating the Web of Things

When implementing Web of Things entities as SmartComponents their in- and outputs are also provided as attributes (see example in Fig. 7). This enables developers to connect WoT entities with other components in the same way as described before. That is, using the proposed *Attribute-Link* for wiring the interfaces. Furthermore, this is not restricted to connecting WoT entities only among themselves. They can also be connected with other components representing for example, ordinary web services. Doing so facilitates implementing complex workflows among sensors, actors and other web services. WoT entities can thereby act as both sensors and/or actors. The example in Fig. 7 shows how a SmartComponent can be used to control a lamp. While the lamp is connected to a bridge using the open protocol ZigBee[7], the bridge itself can be controlled using HTTP. By exposing values like color and brightness using the proposed *Attribute-Link*, the component–and therefore the lamp–can easily be controlled through other SmartComponents.

In the next section, we give a detailed insight of our practical contribution to the *Rapid Mashup Challenge 2016*.

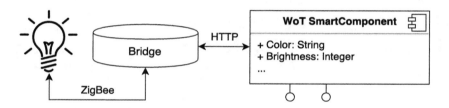

Fig. 7. Light bulb control as SmartComponent bridging different protocols

4   Demonstration

In this section, we give a detailed summary of our demonstration of the Smart-Composition approach at the *Rapid Mashup Challenge 2016* in companion to the ICWE2016 in Lugano, Switzerland. We start with an outline of the presented mashup, followed by a breakdown of activities that were done in preparation of the challenge. Finally, we describe the actual steps for creating the mashup and the demo flow.

4.1   The Presented Mashup

Within our live demonstration, we presented an implementation of the first motivation scenario "media enrichment", we described at the beginning. A screenshot of an example state of the entire mashup composition can be seen in Fig. 8.

---

[7] http://www.zigbee.org/zigbee-for-developers/zigbee3-0/.

Fig. 8. Screenshot of the presented "media enrichment" mashup

We use a video player as the central point and beginning of the information flow. Next to the playing video, several other components displaying different kinds of information are arranged. We show geographical locations on a Google map as well as their current temperature, list related videos on YouTube, show descriptions of things from Wikipedia, display tweets and images about a topic, connect a light bulb to represent the videos average color and show the latest news from the New York Times. We offer multiple ways to interact with the mashup application, like selecting other videos, manually entering locations or rearranging the components.

4.2 Preparation of the Challenge

As part of the preparation of the challenge, we created several SmartComponents as stand-alone building blocks for our mashup. Some of them were already implemented, some we specifically created for the demonstration. To present a complex and also interactive mashup scenario, we prepared the following Smart-Components: Smart-Video, Translate-Text, Semantic-Extraction, Simple-Chart,

Twitter-Tweets, Wikipedia-Extract, Flickr-Images, Youtube-Search, Google-Map, Google-Geocoder, Nytimes-News and Current-Weather. To integrate the Web of Things we additionally implemented a Philips-Hue component that is capable of controlling Philips Hue light bulbs. This will highlight the applicability of our mashup approach for the integration of environmental actors and sensors. As described in Sect. 3, all components can be configured and interlinked using attributes. To realize the mashup idea at best, we designed an information flow that ideally makes use of the single SmartComponents' functions. A detailed description of this demo flow is given in the following section.

4.3   The Demo Flow

To give an insight of how we realized the mashup scenario, how components are interlinked and what information is used, we cover a part of the whole demo flow in detail. The demonstration starts with a central component that is producing information while other components mostly consume, process and/or visualize it. In our example scenario the first producing component is a video with subtitles attached that is realized using our Smart-Video element. The Smart-Video element can be configured with, for example, a YouTube video URI and provides its subtitles as time-based information during playback using an attribute as the external interface. Since the single subtitles are annotated with timestamps, they can be provided only when they are relevant to the current video scene. As displayed in listing 7, the *Smart-Video* element is configured with the YouTube URL *https://www.youtube.com/watch?v=507ajur4eLo*, which is defined in the static HTML markup of the mashup. The other three attributes *current-time*, *current-color* and *text_de* are output interfaces that dynamically provide information. The one that is firstly used within our demo flow is the *text_de* attribute. This attribute value represents the current's scene subtitle. Since it is in German language in our example, it is labeled *text_de*. Thus, the initial state of the mashup will be just a playing video that offers textual information.

The flow continues by connecting the Smart-Video component to another one called *Translate-Text*. This component is capable of translating text from one language to another one. Again, the component is added to the HTML markup of the mashup.

```
<smart-video
    youtube-url="https://www.youtube.com/watch?v=507ajur4eLo"
    current-time="110.313304"
    current-color="#78534c"
    text_de="Ein besonderer Tipp ist [...]">
</smart-video>
```

Listing 7. Configured Smart-Video component in markup

To connect both component, we use our proposed *Attribute-Link* component. This component can be added either by directly specifying it in the markup or by

Fig. 9. "Attribute Linker" overlay after a source component was selected

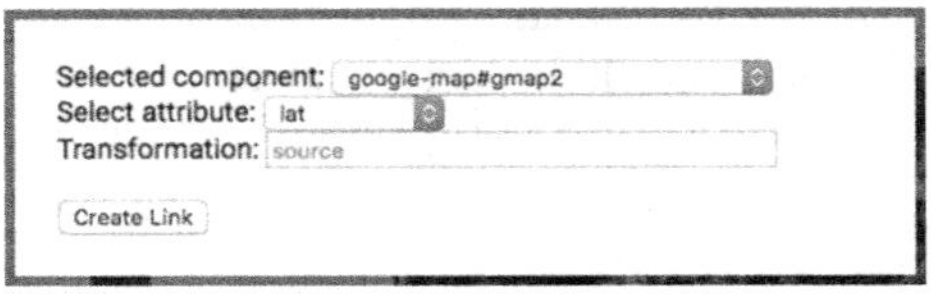

Fig. 10. "Attribute Linker" overlay after a target component was selected

using the UI assistance called "Attribute Linker" we provide as shown in Figs. 9 and 10. The "Attribute Linker" can be accesses using the buttons available at the top of our mashup (see Fig. 8) and automatically creates the *Attribute-Link* element with the required configuration after the user has selected source and target components using the mouse. The resulting markup should then look like as stated in listing 8.

```
<attribute-link
    source="smart-video@text_de"
    target="translate-text@text">
</attribute-link>
```

Listing 8. Attribute-Link from Smart-Video to Translate-Text

This will then enable the propagation of the German subtitles of the video to the translation components input interface called *text*. The translated text is provided through the attribute *translated-text* and can again be used by other components (see listing 9).

```
<translate-text
    from="de"
    to="en"
    text="Ein besonderer Tipp ist [...]"
    translated-text="A special tip is [...]">
</translate-text>
```

Listing 9. Markup of the Translate-Text SmartComponent

To supply the mashup with more meaningful information, we provide a *Semantic-Extraction* component. This component exploits the API of *AlchemyAPI*[8] and extracts entities from text that are automatically categorized.

---

[8] https://www.alchemyapi.com/.

Using this categorization the component can provide lists of entities as output values as it is shown in listing 11. A useful category to start with is the *location* type, where all recognized geographic places are listed.

```
<attribute-link
    source="translate-text@translated-text"
    target="semantic-extraction@text">
</attribute-link>
```

Listing 10. Attribute-Link from Translate-Text to Semantic-Extraction

```
<semantic-extraction
    text="A special tip is the [...]"
    term="['Enoteca delle ALPI']"
    location="['Sondrio']"
    person="[]"
    organization="[]">
</semantic-extraction>
```

Listing 11. Markup of the Semantic-Extraction SmartComponent

Since we can not directly display a named place on a map that only takes geographic coordinates as input, we need another data transformation component. Therefore, we use our *Google-Geocoder* component that has an input attribute called *address* and geocodes this into geographical coordinates that are provided as *lat* and *lng* values (cf. listing 13). Again, we apply the *Attribute-Link* to connect both components. As the location entities are provided as an array of values, the transformation option is used to select only the first entry (see listing 12).

```
<attribute-link
    source="semantic-extraction@location"
    target="google-geocoder@address"
    transformation="(JSON.parse(source))[0]">
</attribute-link>
```

Listing 12. Attribute-Link from Semantic-Extraction to Google-Geocoder with transformation function provided

```
<google-geocoder
    address="Sondrio"
    lat="46.1698583"
    lng="9.878767400000015">
</google-geocoder>
```

Listing 13. Markup of the Google-Geocoder SmartComponent

Thus, the final data flow of the previously described excerpt of the whole mashup will be as displayed in Fig. 11. The necessary actions for adding more

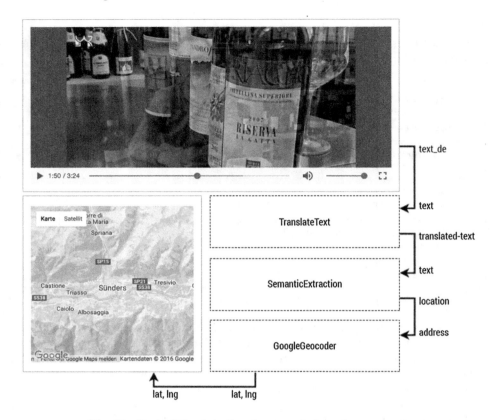

Fig. 11. Part of the data flow in presented mashup scenario

components to the mashup – *adding a SmartComponent and connecting it to another one using an Attribute-Link* – are repeated for all the other mentioned SmartComponents.

For the demonstration of the integration of the Web of Things, we showcase a Philips Hue light bulb in our live demo. This light bulb is also controlled by a mashup component. Besides turning the light bulb on and off, we connect it to the *Smart-Video* element, which offers a *current-color* interface that represents the average color of the current video frame. Doing the former creates an environmental light that harmonizes with the video content.

While not limiting the user experience to a single screen, we additionally demonstrate the distribution of the mashup to multiple devices. Thus, any SmartComponent can be moved to another connected device and will still be able to receive updated information if the mashup was properly configured. Therefore, we set up a *Messaging-Server* and pre-configured a *Messaging-Service* component as shown in listing 14. All *Attribute-Link* components that are created using the "Attribute Linker" are also placed within the *Messaging-Service* scope and therefore also applied to remote components.

```
<messaging-service
    endpoint="http://vsr-demo.informatik.tu-chemnitz.de:9009"
    session="mashup-challenge">
        <attribute-link [...]></attribute-link>
</messaging-service>
```

Listing 14. Configured Messaging-Service with endpoint and session

Demonstration. The demonstrated mashup is available for live testing at: http://myvsr.eu/demo/rmc/

5 Related Work

Mashups have been topic of research for some years now. Daniel et al. presented a comprehensive overview of mashup approaches in [2,4]. Furthermore, the last years Rapid Mashup Challenge proceedings [3] give an interesting insight of current mashup tools.

The mashup concept is not limited to user interface mashups, there is also a special focus on data integration. Yahoo! Pipes[9] (not available anymore), for instance, is an approach that provides only data-oriented composition. Thus, it only processes data (RSS/Atom feeds or XML/JSON resources) as input and also provides data as output. The processing itself is done using a pipeline consisting of multiple components. It is possible to integrate data from various sources, which can then be manipulated and passed to further processing units until the transformation is completed. This pipeline consists of various components that are offering different options for manipulating and processing data and can be combined freely. Additionally, Pipes offers querying web services to include new functionalities.

Other tools like JackBe Presto[10] are comprehensive mashup platforms targeting enterprises. Presto offers the creation, testing and deployment of dynamic applications using various data sources. It particularly allows to use common data sources used in the business sector, like Excel sheets or Oracle data, which is often not supported by other tools. The composition of mashups can also be performed by inexperienced users with the assistance of the Presto Wires tool. More complex compositions can be described using the EMML language, which requires expert knowledge. Presto enables merging data from external and internal sources as well as visualization of the output as a mashlet. Those mashlets can be included in a dashboard, portal or web page.

Microsoft Popfly (discontinued) is a representative of the user interface mashup approach. Popfly offers a visual development environment for the creation of applications based on components (blocks). These blocks can be arranged by dragging and dropping them onto a design area where they can also be connected graphically. Each block provides input and output ports and can

---

[9] http://iphone.pipes.yahoo.com/pipes/.
[10] http://mdc.jackbe.com/prestodocs/v3.0/.

be for example, a gateway to an external service or provide some internal functions. Furthermore, blocks can also graphical display the output of a processing. The communication is done using an event-driven approach. The layout of the application is defined by placing the blocks on the page. The look of the blocks themselves can be modified by inserting HTML, CSS and JavaScript code. Popfly provides a large set of components, like map-based elements, RSS readers or service connectors. Created mashups can be stored and shared on a separate section of the platform.

Inter Mash Maker[11] follows a different approach by integrating data from annotated web pages utilizing a browser plug-in. Once a web page has been annotated, Mash Maker can extract the annotated data and provide it for other components. The annotation is supported by a Structure Editor. The annotions are stored at the Mash Maker Server to share them with other users. The composition itself follows a copy-and-paste paradigm that enables the merging of parts of webpages into another one. The mashup is created only on client side by using the plug-in.

Another user interface mashup approach similar to Mash Maker is Multi-Masher [7]. MultiMasher is a visual tool for multi-device mashups using a direct manipulation interface where a user can select existing UI elements and send them to connected devices. There, the elements will be mashed up with the content that has been sent.

When only taking the aspect of the components into account there is also some work to mention. The W3C created a standard for widgets in the web called W3C Widgets or Packaged Web Apps [13]. Unfortunately, they need to be executed in special platform environments, such as Apache Rave[12] or Apache Shindig[13] and therefore the acceptance and usage is limited. They provide encapsulation by running in iFrames and can exploit inter-widget-communication features for composing applications like mashups. The integration of OpenAjax Hub[14] into Apache Rave is an approach to achieve communication between those widgets. The DireWolf framework [9] is one solution that integrates multi-device communication into the Apache Shindig platform.

There are also component approaches for the client-side web that also suffer from limitations in terms of composition. jQuery, for example, provides a plug-in system that enables developers to create extended HTML elements. In most cases the instantiation and configuration is done by selecting the desired element and applying the provided plug-in constructor to it. Elements are inserted in the document's DOM and therefore are not encapsulated. Communication features are not included. Dojo focuses on a more comprehensive approach and provides a UI library called Dijit. Dijit is a widget system layered on top of Dojo. Dojo widgets are instantiated and configured using the "data-dojo-type" and "data-dojo-props" attributes in the HTML markup. The template content in inserted directly in the document's DOM what increases the risk for conflicts.

---

[11] http://intel.ly/1BW2crD.

[12] http://rave.apache.org/.

[13] http://shindig.apache.org/.

[14] http://www.openajax.org/member/wiki/OpenAjax_Hub_2.0_Specification.

6   Conclusion

In this paper, we presented the SmartComposition approach that eases the development of user interface mashups that can be distributed across multiple-screens. By providing a Web standard-based component format called *SmartComponents* that leverages the Polymer framework, we enable easy, declarative component creation. We facilitating mashup creation only using HTML markup and enable the execution of mashups directly in the browser without additional software. The entire instantiation and configuration of all components as well as the configuration of the inter-component communication is done only in HTML markup. Our *Messaging-Server* in combination with our *Messaging-Service* on the client side enables developers to easily extend mashups to be multi-screen-capable.

In the Rapid Mashup Challenge, we demonstrated the practical applicability of our approach. We showed a complex media enrichment mashup that used multiple user interface as well as data transformation components to create an extensive user experience. We also integrated elements of the Web of Things and mashed up real-world things with the Web.

Future research will address the extension of the distributed inter-component communication in terms of more fine-grained control, for example, targeting specific devices. Furthermore, we want to work on a visual editor for SmartComposition mashups.

7   Feature Checklist

Mashup Type	Hybrid mashups
Component Types	Data, Logic &UI components
Runtime Location	Both Client and Server
Integration Logic	Choreographed integration
Instantiation Lifecycle	Short-living
Targeted End-User	Local Developers
Automation Degree	Manual
Liveness Level	Level 4
Interaction Technique	Editable Example
Online User Community	None

References

1. Chudnovskyy, O., Fischer, C., Gaedke, M., Pietschmann, S.: Inter-Widget Communication by Demonstration in User Interface Mashups. In: Daniel, F., Dolog, P., Li, Q. (eds.) ICWE 2013. LNCS, vol. 7977, pp. 502–505. Springer, Heidelberg (2013). doi:10.1007/978-3-642-39200-9_45
2. Daniel, F., Matera, M.: Mashups: Concepts Models and Architectures. Data-Centric Systems and Applications. Springer, Heidelberg (2014)
3. Daniel, F., Pautasso, C.: Rapid Mashup Development Tools: First International Rapid Mashup Challenge, RMC 2015, Rotterdam, The Netherlands, June 23, 2015. Revised Selected Papers. CCIS, Springer (2016)

4. Daniel, F., Soi, S., Casati, F.: From Mashup Technologies to Universal Integration: Search Computing the Imperative Way. In: Ceri, S., Brambilla, M. (eds.) Search Computing. LNCS, vol. 5950, pp. 72–93. Springer, Heidelberg (2010). doi:10.1007/978-3-642-12310-8_5

5. Guinard, D., Trifa, V.: Building the Web of Things: With examples in Node.js and Raspberry Pi. Manning Publications, Shelter Island, New York (2016)

6. Guinard, D., Trifa, V., Mattern, F., Wilde, E.: From the Internet of Things to the Web of Things: Resource-Oriented Architecture and Best Practices. In: Uckelmann, D., Harrison, M., Michahelles, F. (eds.) Architecting the Internet of Things, pp. 97–129. Springer, Heidelberg (2011). doi:10.1007/978-3-642-19157-2_5

7. Husmann, M., Nebeling, M., Norrie, M.C.: MultiMasher: A Visual Tool for Multi-Device Mashups. In: Sheng, Q.Z., Kjeldskov, J. (eds.) ICWE 2013. LNCS, vol. 8295, pp. 27–38. Springer, Heidelberg (2013). doi:10.1007/978-3-319-04244-2_4

8. Kopetz, H.: Internet of Things. Real-time Systems. Springer, Heidelberg (2011)

9. Kovachev, D., Renzel, D., Nicolaescu, P., Klamma, R.: DireWolf - Distributing and Migrating User Interfaces for Widget-Based Web Applications. In: Daniel, F., Dolog, P., Li, Q. (eds.) ICWE 2013. LNCS, vol. 7977, pp. 99–113. Springer, Heidelberg (2013). doi:10.1007/978-3-642-39200-9_10

10. Krug, M., Wiedemann, F., Gaedke, M.: SmartComposition: A Component-Based Approach For Creating Multi-Screen Mashups. In: Casteleyn, S., Rossi, G., Winckler, M. (eds.) ICWE 2014. LNCS, vol. 8541, pp. 236–253. Springer, Heidelberg (2014). doi:10.1007/978-3-319-08245-5_14

11. Krug, M., Wiedemann, F., Gaedke, M.: SmartComposition: Extending Web Applications to Multi-Screen Mashups. In: Daniel, F., Pautasso, C. (eds.) RMC 2015. CCIS, vol. 591, pp. 50–62. Springer, Heidelberg (2016). doi:10.1007/978-3-319-28727-0_4

12. Web Hypertext Application Technology Working Group (WHATWG): HTML Standard - The template element (2016). https://html.spec.whatwg.org/multipage/scripting.html#the-template-element

13. World Wide Web Consortium (W3C), Cáceres, M: Packaged Web Apps (Widgets) - Packaging and XML Configuration (2012). https://www.w3.org/TR/widgets/

14. World Wide Web Consortium (W3C), Denicola, D: Custom Elements - W3C Working Draft (2016). https://www.w3.org/TR/custom-elements/

15. World Wide Web Consortium (W3C), Glazkov, D., Morrita, H: HTML Imports - W3C Working Draft (2016). https://www.w3.org/TR/html-imports/

16. World Wide Web Consortium (W3C), Ito, H: Shadow DOM - W3C Working Draft (2016). https://www.w3.org/TR/shadow-dom/

Linked Widgets Platform for Rapid Collaborative Semantic Mashup Development

Tuan-Dat Trinh$^{(\boxtimes)}$, Peter Wetz, Ba-Lam Do, Elmar Kiesling, and A. Min Tjoa

TU Wien, Vienna, Austria
{tuan.trinh,peter.wetz,ba.do,elmar.kiesling,a.tjoa}@tuwien.ac.at

Abstract. In recent years, data has become vital in supporting our everyday lives. Along with large volumes of open data available on the web, various types of public, private, and enterprise data are stored in the cloud or distributed over multiple devices. The value of this data would increase drastically if we were able to integrate it. This would enable more sophisticated presentation and analysis of previously disparate data. So far, however, it is challenging for non-expert users to efficiently make use of such data because (i) *data heterogeneity* hampers integration of different kinds of data that are stored in various formats and spread among storage infrastructures; (ii) manual data integration processes are typically neither *reproducible*, nor *reusable*; and (iii) the lack of support for *exploration* does not allow for the integration of *arbitrary data sources*. This paper tackles these challenges by introducing a mashup platform that combines semantic web and mashup concepts to help users obtain insights and make informed decisions. To this end, we leverage a semantic model of mashup components for automated techniques that support the user in exploring available data. Moreover, we introduce a collaborative and distributed model to create and execute mashups. This facilitates distributed ad-hoc integration of heterogeneous data contributed by multiple stakeholders.

1 Context and Goals

Due to the evolution of the web, services, and a large number of smart devices, we can now access and make use of various kinds of data to support everyday decision making. On the one hand, large volumes of open data have been made publicly available covering many topics and aspects. Open data has the potential to create new insights and support informed decisions. Adopted by the G8 in 2013, the Open Data Charter[1] reflects the growing importance of open government data. The charter stipulates that open data must be discoverable, accessible, and usable by all people. On the other hand, we may possess private data which should not be seen by the public. Both open and private data can be stored in the cloud or on our own devices, such as mobile phones or desktop computers.

---

[1] https://www.gov.uk/government/publications/open-data-charter/
g8-open-data-charter-and-technical-annex (accessed October 7, 2016).

© Springer International Publishing AG 2017
F. Daniel and M. Gaedke (Eds.): RMC 2016, CCIS 696, pp. 51–73, 2017.
DOI: 10.1007/978-3-319-53174-8_4

Data integration offers a new view on data and helps us to explore and reveal useful information hidden in and spread among multiple data sources. There are many scenarios that demonstrate the value of data integration. However, it is challenging for end users to make effective use of available isolated datasets, because (i) *data heterogeneity* hampers the integration of different kinds of data that are stored in various formats such as CSV, XML, JSON, or RDF and spread among various storage infrastructures (e.g., databases, files, cloud, personal computers, mobile phones); (ii) manual data integration processes that users perform to collect, clean, enrich, integrate, and visualize data are typically neither *reproducible*, nor *reusable*; (iii) the lack of support for *exploration* does not allow for the integration of *arbitrary data sources*; (iv) there is a lack of means for the *identification* of relevant data sources and meaningful ways to *automatically integrate them.*

Gathering data from multiple sources and performing data analysis, integration, and visualization tasks is hence a cumbersome process. End users cannot, yet, tap the full potential of available datasets, but rather have to rely on custom applications tailored to specific use cases or domains. This further inhibits integrated use of these data. Our goal is to address the discussed issues and enable non-expert users to collaboratively integrate data and obtain new insights.

To this end, this paper introduces a mashup platform in which semantic web and mashup concepts are combined to facilitate data integration for non-expert users in a flexible and efficient manner. We separate complex data integration tasks into reusable modular functions, which are encapsulated in high-level user interface blocks, i.e., the so called Linked Widgets. Based on that, users lacking programming skills can visually connect widgets to create mashup-based data integration applications. We lift non-semantic data to a semantic level at runtime and add explicit semantics to the input and output data of Linked Widgets. Thus we enable users to link disparate data sources, address data heterogeneity, and enrich data from one source with data from other sources to foster new insights.

An innovative aspect of our work is the new model of *semantic, distributed,* and *collaborative* mashups. There is already a body of work related to semantic and collaborative mashups; however, to the best of our knowledge, there is no research on *mashups* assembled from components that are *distributed* among different nodes (e.g., sensors, embedded devices, mobile phones, desktop computers, servers) to collect and integrate data. In our approach, mashup applications can be composed of both *client* and *server* Linked Widgets. *Client widgets* are executed in the local context of a web browser environment. *Server widgets* can be executed as native applications on various platforms, including personal computers, cloud servers, mobile devices, or embedded systems. *Server widgets* can be used to contribute data from the node they are deployed on to one or multiple mashups. They can also make use of the computing resources of its node to continuously process data in the background. This architecture allows stakeholders to expose their private data in a controlled manner by contributing *server widgets* as functional black boxes. This efficiently facilitates collaborative ad-hoc data integration involving multiple stakeholders that contribute data and computing resources.

We have implemented our concepts in a prototype platform, which is available at http://linkedwidgets.org. The data including mashups and semantic models of all widgets is published into the Linked Open Data cloud. It can be accessed via the SPARQL endpoint at http://ogd.ifs.tuwien.ac.at/sparql.

The remainder of this paper is organized as follows. Section 2 discusses related work; Sect. 3 introduces our platform for semantic, distributed, and collaborative mashups; Sect. 4 illustrates the applicability by means of an example use case and Sect. 5 introduces five mashup patterns (i.e., collaborative, persistent, distributed, streaming, and complex mashup pattern) applicable for various use cases. Section 6 concludes the paper with a discussion of findings.

2   Related Work

To facilitate data integration, researchers have been developing mashup-based tools and frameworks for years. Examples include mashArt [2], Intel Mash Maker [4], Microsoft Popfly [7], Exhibit [9], ResEval Mash [10], Apatar[2], MashQL [11], DERI Pipes [13], Information Workbench[3], Husky[4], Vegemite [14], Super Stream Collider [15], Yahoo! Pipes [16], Damia [17], Presto[5], Google Mashup Editor [18], Mashroom [20], and Marmite [21]. Many of them are geared towards end users and allow them to efficiently create applications by connecting simple and light-weight components. Various surveys [1,3,5,6,8] have been conducted to categorize, evaluate, and identify the limitations of these mashup tools.

A limited number of frameworks, such as Super Stream Collider [15], DERI Pipes [13], and MashQL [11], aim at semantic data processing. These frameworks, however, do not leverage semantic web techniques to facilitate automatic data integration for non-expert users [8], neither do they provide mechanisms to integrate semantic with non-semantic data. Thus our objective is first to focus on semantic mashups and overcome the inherent limitations. We therefore design semantic models for mashup components and leverage the semantics to foster mashup-based data exploration and integration. The input data of mashup components can be available in different formats (e.g., CSV, XML, JSON, RDF), but the semantic models impose the semantic format on the output data and hence tackle data heterogeneity.

The surveys show that it is difficult for non-expert users to use the mashup frameworks for composition and integration. On the one hand, a high-level and problem-oriented framework is easier to use than a low-level one, because it does not require users to be familiar with special technological and programming concepts. On the other hand, we need a generic framework that can deal

---

[2] http://www.apatar.com/ (accessed October 7, 2016).

[3] http://www.fluidops.com/en/portfolio/information_workbench/ (accessed October 7, 2016).

[4] http://www.husky.fer.hr/ (accessed October 7, 2016).

[5] http://mdc.jackbe.com/enterprise-mashup (accessed October 7, 2016).

with the increasing number of heterogeneous web resources rather than one tailored towards specific problems and resources. These design objectives lead to a trade-off [1]. A versatile mashup framework typically consists of a large number of predefined components; users generally have a clear idea of what they are trying to achieve, but they do not know which components they need and how to correctly combine them in order to reach their goal. This *"simplicity and expressive power"* trade-off [1] is a challenging issue.

The two surveys [1,6] discuss the importance of the communities behind the frameworks in relation to the success of end-user development tools. An open and collaborative model – which ties together three stakeholders (i.e., data publishers, developers, and end users) – enables each stakeholder to contribute and share their work to the open data community. Based on available data sources provided by different data publishers, developers are encouraged to create and deploy mashup components that are free to use or reuse. By combining such components, users can create mashup applications to work with open data in a dynamic and creative manner. The applications finally can be shared or reconfigured among the communities fostering reusability. However, to the best of our knowledge, current research focuses on user communities only and allows them to share, comment, or rank their mashups. There is no mashup-based data integration framework that can facilitate collaborative work among users, data publishers, and developers in order to encourage widespread use of (linked) open data.

The survey [3] discusses the challenge to integrate data that is stored in different devices, but is not available on the web, yet. In the literature so far, there is no research on *mashups* assembled from components that are *distributed* among different nodes (e.g., sensors, embedded devices, mobile phones, desktop computers, servers) to collect and integrate data. Such *distributed mashups* facilitate *collaborative* data integration in which each stakeholder contributes their data and computing resources to the shared processing flow.

3   Proposed Mashup Approach

3.1   Architecture

The Linked Widgets platform architecture is illustrated in Fig. 1. Linked Widgets extend the concept of standard web widgets[6] with explicit semantics. In particular, the semantics of their inputs and outputs as well as of the transformations they perform are explicitly described. Linked Widgets consume and produce Linked Data and may integrate data from sources such as raw data in CSV, XML, JSON, or HTML, data collected from databases, and data fetched from APIs and cloud services.

Based on their execution mode, widgets can be classified as *client* or *server widgets*. From a functional point of view, we can furthermore categorize them into (i) *data widgets*, (ii) *processing widgets*, and (iii) *visualization widgets*. Linked

---

[6] http://www.w3.org/TR/widgets/ (accessed October 7, 2016).

Widgets are highly reusable and can be parameterized to create mashups that contain data, application logic, and presentation layers.

Client widgets are executed on the client side, i.e., they use client memory and processor resources; data is collected and processed at runtime in the browser. The server hosting the *client widgets* is not necessarily the platform server, i.e., a mashup can combine widgets hosted on different servers. This feature makes the platform flexible and allows external parties to host widgets on their own infrastructure. *Client widgets* are easy to develop and necessary for a lightweight and scalable mashup platform. However, their capabilities are restricted by the web browser execution environment.

Server widgets shift the execution function from the browser environment to standalone application environments on desktop computers, mobile phones, tablets, sensor, or embedded systems. *Server widgets* provide the following benefits: (i) They can act as a data connector to obtain and provide data on different services, devices, or systems for a mashup; (ii) they facilitate collaborative use cases where each participant contributes *data* or *processing widgets* to a shared mashup; (iii) because their computing tasks are performed within the hosting devices, similar to *client widgets*, they reduce the platform server load; (iv) they can run persistently in the background to collect or process data for data monitoring or data streaming applications; (v) *server widgets* deployed on powerful servers are capable of processing large volumes of data over extended time periods.

By creating a connection between an output terminal of a widget and an input terminal of another widget, users can model data flows and integrate data without any programming skills. Internally, we use JSON-LD[7] for the exchange of RDF data between widgets.

A web-based *collaborative mashup editor* forms the core of the data integration architecture. Multiple mashup users can compose and execute mashups simultaneously and collaboratively and integrate private data with publicly available data sources. Mashup creators can locate available widgets using *semantic widget search* and group them into collections. They then connect those widgets to build mashups. The platform supports them in this process by suggesting and enforcing valid connections by means of the *terminal matching* module. In addition, the *automatic mashup composition* module can automatically compose a complete mashup from a widget, or a complete branch that consumes or provides data for a specific input or output terminal. Built on top of the *automatic mashup composition* module, the *tag-based automatic composition* module allows users to compose mashups through structured text input.

The resulting mashups fall into three categories: (i) *local mashups*, which consist exclusively of client widgets, (ii) *distributed mashups*, which consist entirely of server widgets, except for the final visualization widget(s), (iii) and *hybrid mashups*, which make use of both client and server widgets. A *local mashup* does not use any resources of the platform server, because it is executed completely inside the client browser. This implies that intermediate and final data

---

[7] http://www.w3.org/TR/json-ld/ (accessed October 7, 2016).

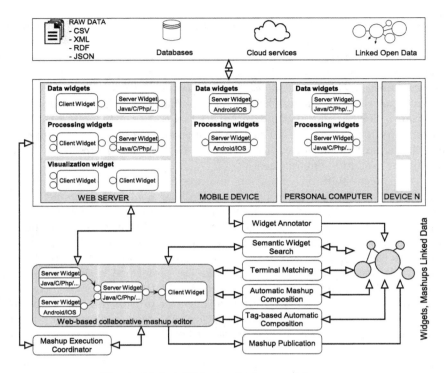

Fig. 1. Linked Widgets platform architecture

are lost as soon as the user closes the web browser. In contrast, widgets in *distributed mashups* are executed remotely as persistent applications; their output can hence be accessed at any time. *Hybrid* and *distributed mashups* can involve multiple nodes, each executing individual server widgets. This is highly useful, for instance, for streaming data scenarios where data must be collected and processed continuously over a longer period of time.

The *mashup execution coordinator* is a key component that enables widgets to communicate. We design *local*, *remote*, and *hybrid* protocols for the three types of mashups. Based on the publish/subscribe model, the protocols facilitate efficient communication between independently developed widgets while minimizing the platform server load.

Complete mashups can be published by users on their website by means of the *mashup publication* module. A published mashup shows the final *visualization widget* only and hides all previous data processing steps from the viewer. The mashup itself can also be encapsulated as a new *data widget*.

For detailed information on client widgets, server widgets, their semantic models, and three protocols that facilitate widget communication during execution please refer to our previous work [19].

3.2 Rapid Mashup Creation

A large and fast-growing number of ready-to-use datasets and services are available; the Linked Widgets platform is not tailored towards particular datasets, but integrates data from arbitrary sources. Available widgets can also be combined with widgets that may become available in the future; currently available data can be merged with future data without modifying existing widgets. The platform facilitates data integration in a rapid and flexible manner as we can simply add or remove a data source to enable new use cases.

First of all, to simplify the mashup development process, based on the explicit input and output semantic model of Linked Widgets, we develop a model matching algorithm (which is implemented in the *Terminal Matching* module) to validate the links between widgets. This allows non-expert users to discover all widgets that can provide data to or consume data from input and output terminals of a widget. Let i and o denote the root nodes of the input and output tree models (cf. [19]), respectively. There are three conditions for matching input and output models: (i) the RDF classes of i and o must be identical, or the RDF class of i must be a subclass of that of o; (ii) any child of i must correspond to a child of o (i.e., the set of properties required by the input must be a subset of properties provided by the output); (iii) recursively, the data model of the input object property must match with the data model of the corresponding output object property.

Leveraging the model matching algorithm, we design an automatic mashup composition algorithm to identify all possible *complete* mashups from a given set of Linked Widgets. A *complete* mashup is a set of widgets and the links between their input and output terminals, such that (i) all links are valid, (ii) all terminals must be wired, and (iii) each output terminal is linked to exactly one input terminal. To this end, in the following, we reduce the mashup composition algorithm to a *find all cycles* algorithm.

From a given set of widgets (e.g., $\{W_1, ...W_7\}$), we construct a directed graph illustrated in Fig. 2. For every processing widget that has n input terminals, we add $(n-1)$ virtual terminals (e.g., V_1^5 is the only virtual terminal of W_5). The vertex set then consists of all input, output, and virtual terminals of all widgets. We need to create virtual terminals to be able to apply the Johnson algorithm which is described in the following.

The edge set consists of four subsets: (i) a set of all valid links E_1 between input and output terminals, which are discovered by the *Terminal Matching* mechanism (e.g., $E_1 = \{(I_1^2,O^1), (I_2^5,O^2), (I_1^5,O^3), (I_1^5,O^4), (I_1^6,O^5), (I_1^7,O^5)\}$); (ii) a set of internal edges E_2 that link input, output, and virtual terminals of every single processing widget (e.g., $E_2 = \{(O^2,I_1^2), (O^4,I_1^4), (O^5,I_1^5), (V_1^5,I_2^5), (O^7,I_1^7)\}$); (iii) a set of edges E_3 that link all output terminals of all data widgets to all virtual terminals (e.g., $E_3 = \{(O^1,V_1^5), (O^3,V_1^5)\}$); and (iv) a set of edges E_4 that link all output terminals of data widgets to all input terminals of all visualization widgets (e.g., $E_4 = \{(O^1,I_1^6), (O^3,I_1^6)\}$).

Next, we can use the Johnson algorithm [12] to identify all cycles of the constructed graph. Its time complexity is bounded by $O((n+e)(c+1))$ and its

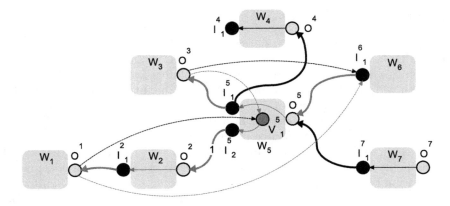

Fig. 2. Example graph corresponds to a set of widgets

space complexity is bounded by $O(n + e)$, where there are n vertices, e edges, and c elementary circuits in the graph. Finally, we apply post-processing steps and return a list of *complete* mashups indentified by the algorithm. For example, the cycle $\{I_1^6, O^5, I_1^5, O^3, V_1^5, I_2^5, O^2, I_1^2, O^1, I_1^6\}$ leads to a complete mashup of five widgets $\{W_1, W_2, W_3, W_5, W_6\}$ by removing all virtual terminals and keeping all edges in the first subset of edges E_1 only. However, the cycle $\{I_1^6, O^5, I_1^5, O^3, I_1^6\}$ does not yield a mashup, because I_2^5 of the involved widget W_5 is unlinked. It will therefore not appear in the final results.

4   Mashup Demo

4.1   Description of the Mashup Demo

For the mashup demonstration, consider the need to integrate data from different Excel and Google spreadsheets in an enterprise context. The typical process to achieve this goal is to download all spreadsheets then copy, delete columns, and create formulas to aggregate the data. These tedious tasks take up a lot of time and have to be repeated whenever the source data changes. To address this issue, we show that the Linked Widgets platform is capable of performing these tasks rapidly, flexibly, collaboratively, and in a distributed manner across groups of users and their multiple devices. The example collects, combines, and visualizes ice-cream sales data from a series of points of sale (POS) and relates it with the weather conditions obtained from the Wunderground API services[8].

To this end, we developed the following Linked Widgets: (i) *Google Sheet:* this client and data widget analyzes a sheet stored in the Google Drive cloud and transforms it into a W3C data cube[9], which is the semantic representation of the input sheet. (ii) *Local Spreadsheet:* this server and data widget runs on a

---

[8] https://www.wunderground.com/ (accessed October 7, 2016).
[9] https://www.w3.org/TR/vocab-data-cube (accessed October 7, 2016).

mobile phone or a desktop computer to collect local data. Similar to the *Google Sheet* widget, it receives a sheet and returns a W3C data cube. It allows users to directly add data from their devices to a mashup without the need to upload data to the web. (iii) *Cube Merger:* this server and processing widget receives a number of W3C data cubes as input, merges them, and outputs a data cube which includes the combined input data. It requires that all input cubes have the same dimensions and measures. (iv) *Aggregation:* based on the semantics of the input cube data, this client and processing widget aggregates data along the dimensions of the input data cube. It supports the aggregation functions *sum* and *average*. It is a generic widget in the sense that its interface is automatically generated based on the input data. (v) *Filter:* this client and processing widget calculates and returns a slice of the input data cube; to this end, users set the fixed values on one or multiple dimensions of the cube. (vi) *Temperature Enrichment:* this client and processing widget uses weather data to automatically enrich its input data cube if the cube contains time-dependent data. The output data is a new cube with temperature added as a new measure for each input date. (vii) *Google Chart:* this visualization widget analyzes the input data cube and displays it in a chart.

4.2 Description of the Preparation Needed to Make Approach Ready for Demo

The mashup demo engages a group of users, that is, the branch managers of the respective POSs. They need a mobile phone, tablet or desktop computer and a web browser to create, access, and run mashups from the platform.

For users who would like to contribute a private spreadsheet to the shared mashup, they need to download the *Local Spreadsheet* widget[10]. In our demo, it is realized as a desktop application. It extends an abstract desktop widget that implements the Linked Widgets protocol to communicate with other widgets. To develop the *Local Spreadsheet* widget, we need to implement the *execution* function only.

4.3 Description of the Demo Flow

The life cycle of a new mashup is initiated by a *host user*, who can then choose from a number of available Linked Widgets (listed in Sect. 4.1) to include in the palette of the mashup. To add a private widget, the user can provide the name and the URL of the widget. Then, after dragging and dropping a widget, she (or other users) can query the platform to (i) list all complete mashups that contain the widget, (ii) construct all possible complete *mashup branches* for a particular input or output terminal of the widget, and (iii) construct all complete *mashup branches* for all input terminals of the widget. A *mashup branch* is a part of a complete mashup that consumes (provides) data for a specific output (input) terminal. These features are available in the user interface via a click on the

---

[10] http://linkedwidgets.org/serverwidgets/ExcelSheet.jar (accessed October 7, 2016).

question mark symbol in the widget bar, and the symbol that appears when we hover a terminal.

The first example mashup involves three Austrian POSs, which are located in Vienna, Graz, and Linz, respectively. Data are stored in two types of Google spreadsheet: (i) a point of sale spreadsheet that contains id, name, latitude, longitude, city, country of the POS; and (ii) three sales spreadsheets, each listing the number of items sold per day per category at that point of sale. Whereas the point of sale spreadsheet is provided by the *host user*, the three sale spreadsheets of POS *A*, *B*, *C* are provided by the local branch managers, who update the data every day by adding new rows into the spreadsheet.

The *host user* first adds a *Google Sheet*, a *Cube Merger*, a *Filter*, an *Aggregation*, and a *Google Chart* widget and links their input and output terminals. She then sends an automatically generated token that identifies the mashup instance to everyone in the group. Then, the recipients enter the token to load the respective mashup instance and start working collaboratively. All operations such as adding (removing) a widget to (from) the mashup, connecting widgets, resizing a widget, etc. are propagated and synchronized into all editors.

As soon as every local branch manager drags and drops their *Google Sheet* widget and connects it with the *Cube Merger* widget, the *host user* runs the last widget of the mashup, which is the *Google Chart* widget in our example. The three managers now enter the link to their *Google Sheet* widget; Fig. 3 illustrates the mashup shown on the screen of the manager of POS *A*. As soon as she executes her *Google Sheet* widget, everyone in the group can immediately see the updated data in the chart. An arbitrary participant can remove her widget and leave the collaborative mashup group, or the host user can invite additional users to join the group.

In this example mashup, the options inside the *Filter* and *Aggregation* widgets are generated automatically based on the input data cube. By changing the automatically generated options inside the *Filter* and *Aggregation* widgets, different types of analyses can be quickly performed. For example, collaborators can "compare all-time sales of all POS", "compare sales of all POS in 2014", "compare sales of fruit, milk, and chocolate items of POS *A* in 2014", "compare aggregate sales in different countries or cities", or "compare sales of fruit items in different cities" as shown in Fig. 3.

Because Linked Widgets within a mashup can be contributed and executed by multiple independent actors, it is important to log the contribution of each to the resulting integrated data. We therefore store provenance data when a mashup is executed. The provenance data contains information about each widget's contribution to the final result. The generated provenance trail includes information on who executed a particular widget, the timestamps when processing started and finished, etc. The provenance is shown when users press the download button in the widget bar. For example, part of provenance of the *Google Sheet* widget contributed by the host user (e.g., Alice) is shown in Listing 1; she acts on the behalf of the developer of the widget to produce a data cube; the data is associated with a signature for reproducibility checking.

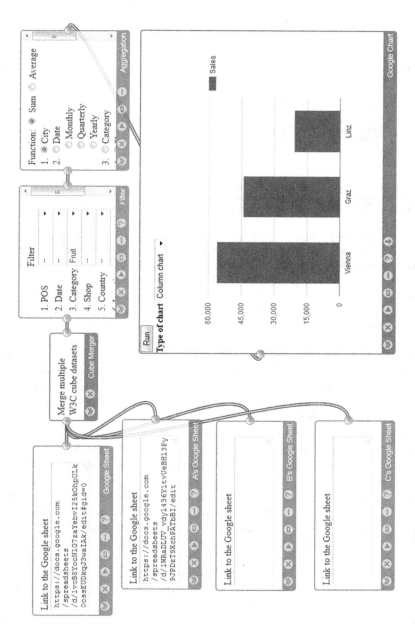

Fig. 3. Collaborative mashup shown on the screen of the manager of Point of Sale A

```
{
    "@context": {...},
    "@type": ["prov:Entity", "void:Dataset"],
    "@id": "http://.../ontology/resource/62e2ba4f9abc75a2b7f1f87cdfeac7b3",
    "signature": "62e2ba4f9abc75a2b7f1f87cdfeac7b3",
    "wasAttributedTo": {
        "@id": "http://linkedwidgets.org/ontology/resource/userAlice",
        "actedOnBehalfOf": {"@id": "http://.../resource/unitProviderDat"}
    },
    "wasGeneratedBy": {
        "@id": "http://.../Execution-nicOtMWOHs",
        "@type": ["prov:Activity", "http://.../ProcessingUnitExecution"],
        "startedAtTime": "Sun August 21 2016 02:06:22 GMT+0200",
        "endedAtTime": "Sun August 21 2016 02:06:23 GMT+0200",
        "hasParameter": [
            {
                "@type": "http://linkedwidgets.org/ontology/Parameter",
                "@id": "_:n1",
                "name": "txtLink",
                "value": "https://docs.google.com/spreadsheets/..."
            }
        ],
        ...
    }
}
```

Listing 1. Provenance for execution of the host user's Google Sheet widget

The sales data can be obtained either from a cloud storage service (e.g. Google Drive), or it originates from a diverse set of devices. For example, in Fig. 4, rather than using Google sheets, the three managers now add local spreadsheets stored on their local computers since they do not want to upload the files to the web (e.g., as sales data is sensitive). Next, each manager selects the file and runs his *Local Spreadsheet* widget (cf. Fig. 5) as a standalone application on his desktop computer. This server widget then generates a URL of his private widget so that the user can add it to the collaborative mashup. Whenever the user modifies his spreadsheet, he re-executes his *Local Spreadsheet* widget to update the result of the whole mashup. Moreover, in this example, we use a *Temperature Enrichment* widget to combine sales data with weather data and deduce the impact of temperature on sales figures for each POS; Fig. 4 illustrates this setup fruit items of POS *A*.

To facilitate collaborative data integration, we offer the *Delegating* widget (cf. Fig. 6) that can persistently be connected with an instance of a server widget. When we run this delegating widget, it subscribes to the *"returning output"* event of the server widget instance whose token is specified in the input box. The delegating widget acts as an agent for the server widget instance, meaning that as soon as the server widget returns its new output data, the delegating widget receives the data and immediately returns the same result.

With the delegating widget, the output data of multiple groups can dynamically be integrated with each other. To this end, each group contributes a *Delegating* widget to a new mashup. Each *Delegating* widget is connected with the last server widget of each group's mashup (i.e., the *Cube Merger* widget in our demo). For example, in Fig. 6, we have three groups (Austria, France, and Italy). The group Austria is described in the previous mashup; it includes three local branch managers from Vienna, Graz, and Linz. As soon as a participant of an arbitrary group (e.g., the Vienna manager) updates his data, the final integrated data collected from all groups in all countries is updated immediately, too.

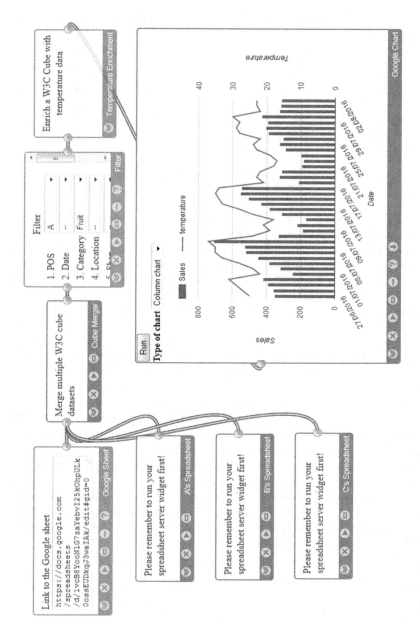

Fig. 4. A mashup composition showing sales data from desktop spreadsheets combined with weather conditions

Fig. 5. Server widget runs as standalone application on a desktop

The *Delegating* widget is designed for collaborative mashups as follows: (i) It first allows a participant to prepare his own data for a collaborative mashup. Rather than exposing a large volume of data, he can extract a relevant part of the data only and perform pre-processing tasks in a private mashup. He then contributes the data to the collaborative group by using a delegating widget. This not only makes data integration more secure (as his data may be sensitive it should not be visible to others), but also speeds up the execution of the whole mashup (as irrelevant parts of data are already removed). The private mashup is not a part of the collaborative mashup, but its final output data is used in the collaborative mashup via the delegating widget. (ii) The delegating widget allows a participant to hide a branch of the collaborative mashup. The Linked Widgets platform enables anyone to develop his own widget; he then can contribute it to the public community or keep it private. A private widget can be used in a collaborative mashup; it is visible to everyone in the shared mashup screen. The hiding feature is hence useful if a participant does not want to expose his private widget used in the collaborative mashup to others. Moreover, it simplifies the overall mashup; each should only see the relevant part of the mashup rather than the part that he can ignore or cannot control.

There are many ways to combine *client widgets* and *server widgets* to develop mashups that are useful for a variety of scenarios. In the next section, we introduce five patterns to compose collaborative, persistent, distributed, streaming, and complex mashups, respectively.

5   Mashup Patterns

5.1   Collaborative Mashups

Definition. A collaborative mashup is a type of mashup application that is edited and/or operated by more than one user at the same time.

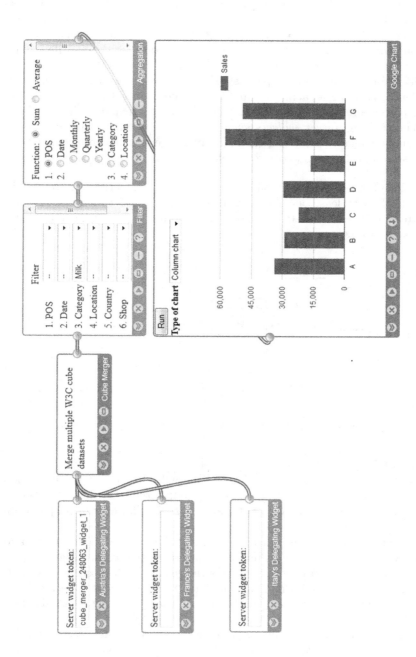

Fig. 6. A Mashup integrating data from three groups

Use Case. Collaborative mashups are useful for a group of users. They can collaboratively define a data processing flow and each participant can supply their input data independently, while all participants immediately get a live representation of the combined data. In this model, tedious and repetitive manual data integration processes (e.g., data cleansing, data uploading, update notifications) are encapsulated in widgets.

Consider, for example, the simple task of scheduling a meeting between users whose calendars are spread across computers, mobile phones, Cloud services, etc. A widget-based collaborative workflow would allow participants to contribute their calendar using *server widgets* such as locally executed Apps or Cloud-based calendar widgets. They can then simply merge their calendar widgets in a collaborative mashup to identify available timeslots.

Pattern. The Linked Widgets collaborative mashup pattern is presented in Fig. 7. It involves at least one server widget (e.g., W) and two users; the two users are responsible for their two widgets (e.g., W_1 and W_2), which can be either client or server widgets.

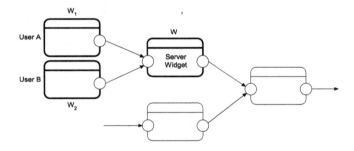

Fig. 7. Collaborative mashup pattern (pattern widgets highlighted with thick borders)

To execute the collaborative mashup, first, an arbitrary participant triggers the run action in the visualization widget. This will also trigger the execution of all preceding widgets (except W_1 and W_2), one after the other. The server widget W, however, cannot run, yet, because it still waits for the output data of W_1 and W_2.

In the next step, the two users set the values of their widget's parameters and run them. As soon as both widgets return output data, the server widget W performs the data integration task and returns the result to its succeeding widget. Whenever W_1 or W_2 submits new output data, the final result is recalculated and immediately presented to every participant in the synchronized visualization widget.

A participant can leave the collaborative mashup at any time. To this end, she removes her widget from the mashup so that the input data of the server widget W is reset, and her private data is removed from the mashup. On the other hand, a new participant can easily join the collaborative mashup by entering the collaborative token to load the mashup and adding her private widget into the collaborative mashup editor.

5.2   Persistent Mashups

Definition. A persistent mashup is a type of mashup application that can continuously run in the background and maintain its status and intermediate data.

Use Case. A persistent mashup can be used for data integration tasks that are typically time-consuming (e.g., statistical analysis, data analysis, and data reporting). To this end, the mashup creator composes a mashup and submits her input data. At any time, she can reopen the mashup to check the current status and result. As she does not host and run the mashup on her device, she can manage a mashup that performs expensive calculation tasks even with a slow client device.

Pattern. Figure 8 shows the Linked Widgets persistent mashup pattern. It contains a server widget placed before a visualization widget, which is a client widget. Because the server widget performs the processing tasks in the respective server rather than the browser environment, it can persistently maintain the calculation data and the intermediate mashup data.

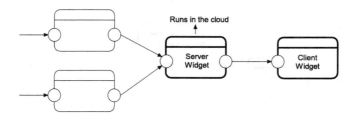

Fig. 8. Persistent mashup pattern

As soon as the mashup is reopened, the client widget requests the latest output data from the server widget for visualization. The browser hence acts as a front-end tool that shows up-to-date data from the back-end processing.

5.3   Distributed Mashups

Definition. A distributed mashup is a type of mashup application in which the involved widgets are hosted in distributed nodes and devices.

Use Case. Distributed mashups facilitate, for instance, integration of sensor data from embedded devices. The data collector tasks run pervasively among the server widgets of distributed nodes. To facilitate data integration, those server widgets can clean, formalize, and convert the data before sending it to a central node where data is aggregated before finally being visualized in a client widget. The distributed model typically involves three types of nodes: (i) embedded devices (which provide input data), (ii) a powerful server (which processes data), and (iii) a personal device such as a mobile phone, tablet, or laptop for visualization. Distributed mashups, moreover, allow us to integrate data from different devices without the necessity to upload the data to a central point.

Pattern. Figure 9 depicts the widget combination pattern of distributed mashups. The involved server widgets are placed in an arbitrary position of the mashup. Based on the available programming language (e.g., Java, Python, Erlang, C++, etc.) of the hosting device, we implement the respective versions of the server widgets. By adding (removing) a widget into (from) a mashup, we can add (remove) the node into (from) the ad-hoc architecture. To this end, it is necessary that the device is connected to the internet so that widgets can communicate using the *remote protocol* (cf. [19]).

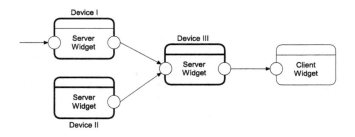

Fig. 9. Distributed mashup pattern

5.4   Streaming Mashups

Definition. A streaming mashup is a type of mashup application in which data flows continuously between two or more widgets.

Use Case. Streaming mashups can, for instance, be used for data monitoring applications. While current data is presented to users, new data is constantly generated, delivered, and aggregated for presentation. Due to the variety of real-time and streaming data sources available on the web (e.g., weather data, public transportation data, data on stock quotes), each can build her own application to process daily data and support decision making. For example, users can compose a mashup that collects the temperature, pressure, and wind speed at different places (e.g., her home, her work place) every minute, based on the weather conditions of the nearest stations. Users can then visualize the aggregated data in a chart, which is updated every minute.

Pattern. The Linked Widgets' streaming mashup pattern is illustrated in Fig. 10. At least one widget continuously runs and returns its output data. We use the term *streaming widget*, which can be either a client or a server widget. A streaming client widget can be used, but the streaming data flow of the mashup will be stopped once we close the browser; a streaming server widget should be used if we intend to make our streaming mashup persistent.

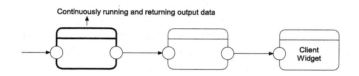

Fig. 10. Streaming mashup pattern

5.5 Complex Mashups

The purpose of classifying hybrid mashup patterns is to clarify and emphasize different aspects of mashups; there is no strict boundary between *collaborative*, *persistent*, *distributed*, and *streaming* mashups. We can combine these types in several ways. For example, we can construct mashups that continuously integrate streaming data from distributed sensors of multiple stakeholders.

6 Conclusions

A large number of data sources, APIs, services, and data visualizations are publicly available. However, non-expert users are not able to directly access, explore, and combine different sources due to their lack of skills and knowledge of data processing.

In this paper, we present a mashup platform for dynamic and automatic exploration and integration of heterogeneous data sources for non-expert users. To foster reusability and creativity, we modularize the functionality into Linked Widgets. Linked Widgets represent modules that users can recombine in order to create new applications. We make use of both client and server computing resources to create a powerful, extensible, and scalable data integration model. With server Linked Widgets, data processing tasks can be run persistently and be distributed among various devices. This is particularly useful for data streaming or data monitoring use cases.

The platform is built upon semantic web concepts. We impose a semantic format on widget outputs. This helps the platform to address data heterogeneity. Based on that, generic widgets such as *Aggregation*, *Filter*, and *Google Chart* can automatically adapt their interface by analyzing the semantics of their input.

We leverage the explicit semantics of Linked Widgets' input and output models to ease and simplify the mashup development process, e.g., by automatically composing meaningful mashups from a given set of available widgets.

Moreover, the platform (i) facilitates collaborative work among users, data publishers, and developers encouraging widespread use of data and (ii) integrates dispersed data stored on different devices and contributed by multiple stakeholders in a rapid manner. Hence, the platform is applicable to a variety of scenarios, such as scientific research, data journalism, enterprise data integration, or ad-hoc integration of web data by non-expert users.

The platform is still in its early stages of development and some limitations apply, which we intend to address in future work. First, we plan to extend the semantic model to include annotation of parameters that can be set in the user interface. Furthermore, we presently focus on collaborative, and distributed data integration scenarios in an open environment. A key issue for future work is to ensure privacy and secure data transfer in order to protect sensitive data. Finally, our research has focused exclusively on conceptual and technical aspects so far; a comprehensive user study as well as extensive performance and scalability testing will provide insights into important applied aspects.

A   Mashup Feature Checklist

Mashup Type

- Data mashups
- Logic mashups
- User Interface (UI) mashups
- **Hybrid mashups**

Component Types

- **Data components**
- **Logic components**
- **UI components**

Runtime Location

- Client-side only
- Server-side only
- **Both Client and Server**

Integration Logic

- UI-based integration
- **Orchestrated integration (local and hybrid mashups)**
- **Choreographed integration (distributed server-side mashups)**

Instantiation Lifecycle

- Stateless
- **Short-living**
- **Long-living (persistent mashups)**

B   Mashup Tool Feature Checklist

Targeted End-User

- Local Developers
- **Non Programmers**
- Expert Programmers

Automation Degree

- **Full Automation**
- **Semi-automation**
- **Manual**

Liveness Level

- Level 1 (Non-Executable Prototype Mockup)
- Level 2 (Explicit Compilation and Deployment Steps)
- **Level 3 (Automatic Compilation and Deployment, requires Re-initialization)**
- Level 4 (Dynamic Modification of Running Mashup)

Interaction Technique

- Editable Example
- Form-based
- Programming by Demonstration
- Spreadsheets
- Textual DSL
- Visual Language (Iconic)
- **Visual Language (Wiring, Implicit Control Flow)**
- Visual Language (Wiring, Explicit Control Flow)
- WYSIWYG
- Natural Language
- Other

Online User Community

- None
- Private
- **Public**

References

1. Aghaee, S., Pautasso, C.: End-user programming for web mashups. In: Harth, A., Koch, N. (eds.) ICWE 2011. LNCS, vol. 7059, pp. 347–351. Springer, Heidelberg (2012). doi:10.1007/978-3-642-27997-3_38

2. Daniel, F., Casati, F., Benatallah, B., Shan, M.-C.: Hosted universal composition: models, languages and infrastructure in mashArt. In: Laender, A.H.F., Castano, S., Dayal, U., Casati, F., Oliveira, J.P.M. (eds.) ER 2009. LNCS, vol. 5829, pp. 428–443. Springer, Heidelberg (2009). doi:10.1007/978-3-642-04840-1_32

3. Di Lorenzo, G., Hacid, H., Paik, H.Y., Benatallah, B.: Data integration in mashups. ACM Sigmod Rec. **38**(1), 59–66 (2009)

4. Ennals, R., Brewer, E., Garofalakis, M., Shadle, M., Gandhi, P.: Intel mash maker: join the web. ACM SIGMOD Rec. **36**(4), 27–33 (2007)

5. Fischer, T., Bakalov, F., Nauerz, A.: An overview of current approaches to mashup generation. In: Proceedings of the International Workshop on Knowledge Services and Mashups (KSM09), pp. 254–259. Citeseer (2009)

6. Grammel, L., Storey, M.A.: An End User Perspective on Mashup Makers. University of Victoria Technical Report DCS-324-IR (2008)

7. Griffin, E.: Foundations of Popfly: Rapid Mashup Development. Apress (2008)

8. Hendrik, A.A., Tjoa, A.M.: Towards semantic mashup tools for big data analysis. In: Linawati, M.M.S., Neuhold, E.J., Tjoa, A.M., You, I. (eds.) ICT-EurAsia 2014. LNCS, vol. 8407, pp. 29–138. Springer, Heidelberg (2014)

9. Huynh, D.F., Karger, D.R., Miller, R.C.: Exhibit: lightweight structured data publishing. In: Proceedings of the 16th International Conference on World Wide Web, pp. 737–746. ACM (2007)

10. Imran, M., Soi, S., Kling, F., Daniel, F., Casati, F., Marchese, M.: On the systematic development of domain-specific mashup tools for end users. In: Brambilla, M., Tokuda, T., Tolksdorf, R. (eds.) ICWE 2012. LNCS, vol. 7387, pp. 291–298. Springer, Heidelberg (2012). doi:10.1007/978-3-642-31753-8_22

11. Jarrar, M., Dikaiakos, M.D.: MashQL: a Query-by-diagram Topping SPARQL. In: Proceedings of the 2nd International Workshop on Ontologies and Information Systems for the Semantic Web, pp. 89–96. ACM (2008)

12. Johnson, D.B.: Finding all the elementary circuits of a directed graph. SIAM J. Comput. **4**(1), 77–84 (1975)

13. Le-Phuoc, D., Polleres, A., Hauswirth, M., Tummarello, G., Morbidoni, C.: Rapid prototyping of semantic mash-ups through semantic web pipes. In: Proceedings of the 18th International Conference on World Wide Web, pp. 581–590. ACM (2009)

14. Lin, J., Wong, J., Nichols, J., Cypher, A., Lau, T.A.: End-user programming of mashups with vegemite. In: Proceedings of the 14th International Conference on Intelligent User Interfaces, pp. 97–106. ACM (2009)

15. Nguyen, M.Q.H., Serrano, M., Le-Phuoc, D., Hauswirth, M.: Super stream collider-linked stream mashups for everyone. In: Proceedings of the Semantic Web Challenge co-located with ISWC 2012. Boston, US (2012)

16. Pruett, M.: Yahoo! Pipes, 1st edn. O'Reilly, Sebastopol (2007)

17. Simmen, D.E., Altinel, M., Markl, V., Padmanabhan, S., Singh, A.: Damia: data mashups for intranet applications. In: Proceedings of the 2008 ACM SIGMOD International Conference on Management of Data, pp. 1171–1182. ACM (2008)

18. Tony, L.: Creating Google Mashups with the Google Mashup Editor. Lotontech Limited (2008)

19. Trinh, T.D., Wetz, P., Do, B.L., Kiesling, E., Tjoa, A.M.: Distributed mashups: a collaborative approach to data integration. IJWIS **11**(3), 370–396 (2015)
20. Wang, G., Yang, S., Han, Y.: Mashroom: end-user mashup programming using nested tables. In: Proceedings of the 18th International Conference on World Wide Web, WWW 2009, pp. 861–870. ACM, New York (2009)
21. Wong, J., Hong, J.I.: Making mashups with marmite: towards end-user programming for the web. In: Proceedings of the SIGCHI Conference on Human Factors in Computing Systems, pp. 1435–1444. ACM (2007)

End-User Development for the Internet of Things: EFESTO and the 5W Composition Paradigm

Giuseppe Desolda[1(✉)], Carmelo Ardito[1], and Maristella Matera[2]

[1] Dipartimento di Informatica, Università degli Studi di Bari Aldo Moro,
Via Orabona, 4, 70125 Bari, Italy
{giuseppe.desolda, carmelo.ardito}@uniba.it
[2] Dipartimento di Elettronica, Informazione e Bioingegneria,
Politecnico di Milano, Piazza Leonardo da Vinci, 32, 20134 Milan, Italy
maristella.matera@polimi.it

Abstract. This paper illustrates a composition paradigm and a related tool to express rules for *smart object composition*. The composition paradigm is characterized by operators for coupling multiple events and conditions exposed by smart objects, and for defining temporal and spatial constraints on rule activation. The design of the composition paradigm is based on the results of an elicitation study that involved 25 participants.

Keywords: End-User Development of mashups · Visual paradigms for ECA rule expression · Internet of Thing

1 Introduction

In the last years, thanks to the spreading of low-cost technologies integrating sensors and actuators, it became possible to build easily the so-called *smart objects*. A smart object is an electronic device connected to Internet, which integrates sensors to feel the environment and/or actuators to communicate with the environment [1]. The proliferation of such devices fostered the born of the Internet of Things (IoT), a novel paradigm where the Internet is connected to the physical world via ubiquitous sensors[1]. The IoT is breeding grounds for different research areas since challenges related to fields like energy consumption, communication protocols, programming languages and end-user development need to be addressed. In this context, many efforts are being devoted to improve technological aspects. Little attention has been instead dedicated to social and practical aspects: despite all the advances in the IoT field, end users still encounter many difficulties when trying to make sense of such technology. The research community agrees on the fact that the opportunities offered by IoT can be amplified if high-level abstractions and adequate interaction paradigms are devised to enable also **non-programmers** to customize and synchronize the behaviour of smart objects [2].

---

[1] http://www.rfidjournal.com/articles/view?4986.

© Springer International Publishing AG 2017
F. Daniel and M. Gaedke (Eds.): RMC 2016, CCIS 696, pp. 74–93, 2017.
DOI: 10.1007/978-3-319-53174-8_5

This paper illustrates an approach that goes in this direction as it offers a visual interaction paradigm that allows end users to express rules for the composition of smart objects. The paradigm is based on a model, called *5W*, which defines some specification constructs (*Which, What, When, Where, Why*) to build rules coupling multiple events and conditions exposed by smart objects, and for defining temporal and spatial constraints on rule activation and actions execution. Such paradigm has been designed during an elicitation study involving 25 participants [3]. It has then been implemented in a Web composition environment that extends the capability of EFESTO, a platform for the End-User Development (EUD) of Web mashups through which data provided by Web APIs can be integrated into unified visualizations [4, 5].

This paper illustrates the composition paradigm and explains how the visual expression of rules by the end users is automatically translated into running code governing the synchronization of the behaviour of multiple objects. The paper is organized as follows. Starting from the analysis of related works, Sect. 2 illustrates the motivations behind our approach. Section 3 then introduces the main elements of the 5W model and by means of a scenario describes the related composition paradigm. Section 4 describes the implementation of the EFESTO platform, also with reference to the feature checklist adopted during the Rapid Mashup Challenge to classify the different mashup frameworks. Section 5 discusses the level of maturity of the platform, by illustrating the evolution of the platform from a tool for data integration to an environment also supporting task automation. Section 6 illustrates the demo given for the challenge. Finally, Sect. 7 concludes the paper also outlining our future work.

2 Related Work

To bring close end users' desire to customize smart objects' behavior and the intrinsic complexity of programming languages, different solutions are emerging. Since a smart object is remotely available as a Web service, in many cases such solutions are getting inspiration from the mashup research area. Mashup tools are Web platforms that permit to access and compose heterogeneous resources, including Web services, by exploiting visual mechanisms [6]. Starting from the mashup approaches, *task automation platforms* [7] have been proposed as means for synchronizing services and smart objects. Such tools support users in the automation of their processes by establishing channels among smart objects (e.g., each time a user enters into his home, the Wi-Fi router switch on). A popular task automation platform is IFTTT (IF This Then That): it provides wizard mechanisms for creating automation rules, called *recipes*, to throw an action on a service when an event is triggered by another service [8]. For instance, when an intrusion is detected by the home alarm system, the Smartwatch shows a notification to the user.

The wizard paradigm fits very well the mental model of non-technical end-users [9], and this is the reason why it is widely exploited also by other task automation tools. An example is *elastic.io*, a tool to create rule expressing data-flow chains [10]. It is more devoted to business aspects and offers the possibility to integrate custom services. Another example is *Zapier*, whose main features are *(i)* the possibility to create rules with multiple events and actions and *(ii)* the use of *filters* on the triggering events to control rules activation [11]. Task automation tools implementing wizard approaches are also available as mobile apps. *Atooma* is one of the most popular; it allows the creation of rules with multiple events and actions, which put into communication device functions, Web services and smart objects [12]. A recent work demonstrated that, even if Atooma supports the creation of very expressive rules, the wizard approach guarantees similar performances between IFTTT (the mobile version) and Atooma with reference to time and accuracy [13]. Similarly to Atooma, tools like *AutomateIt* and *Tasker* support the creation of rules, but they simply enable the composition of apps and functions available on mobile devices [14, 15].

Besides the wizard-based task automation tools, there are other different composition paradigms. For example, the graph metaphor is used to represent a Web service as a node and connections among Web services as "wires". Users can define object communication/behavior by graphically sketching the wires among the objects. A popular tool implementing the wired paradigm is *Node-RED* [16]. Besides offering a set of pre-defined services, it allows users to register personal smart objects by invoking their RESTful interfaces. In addition, Node-RED supports the creation of complex automation rules characterized by: *(i)* multiple services that trigger events and multiple services that react by performing actions; *(ii)* special nodes, used for example to control the communication flow among services by means of custom JavaScript code; *(iii)* debug function to simulate and check the rules under creation. However, such features often require technical skills and thus they are not adequate for non-technical people [17–19]. The wire paradigm is implemented by tools typically devoted to more technical users, for example by *Bip.io* [20] and *Spacebrew* [21].

A completely different paradigm is implemented in *Zipato*, a platform specific for smart objects in domotic systems [22]. The rule creation occurs in a workspace where people can compose puzzle pieces representing components for control flow, sensors and actuators, logical operators, variables and advanced features. Despite the high degree of rule customization, the puzzle metaphor makes Zipato promising for non-technical users. A recent systematic literature review identifies the best software tools that allow end users to manage and configure the behaviors of a smart home [23]. Some of the identified tools were also compared on the basis of seven design principles proposed for smart home control.

The analysis of the previous tools highlighted some lacks that make it difficult for non-programmers to use them effectively. In particular, very often the adopted graphical notations for rule specification do not match the mental model of most users [24]. Research on Web mashup composition paradigms – a field that has many aspects in common with smart object composition – showed that graph-based notations are suitable for programmers, while some issues concerning the conceptual understanding of such notations arise with laypeople who do not think about "connecting" services [17, 19, 25].

Another lack is related to the expressive power of the ECA rules that can be specified, which is limited to simple synchronized behaviors. In [26] authors discuss the importance of temporal and spatial conditions to create ECA rules to better satisfy users' needs. Specifying temporal conditions also emerged as an important requirement in home automation to schedule rule for appliance activation [27]. Some tools allow the definition of such conditions only by means of workarounds, for example by considering additional events to monitor the system time, or by creating filters on smart device data (e.g., in Zapier). Obviously, such workarounds complicate the rule creation, thus resulting into a scarce adoption of the available tools, especially by non-technical users, or in their adoption only for very simple tasks. The following sections will show how the EFESTO platform was extended to alleviate these issues.

3 EFESTO and Its 5W Composition Paradigm

In this section, we describe the 5W composition paradigm and we illustrate its main features through a usage scenario inspired to the live demo given during the ICWE 2016 rapid mashup challenge.

3.1 The 5W Model to Support Rule Definition

The 5W composition paradigm aims to support users without technical skills in computer programming in creating task automation rules that can satisfy a wide range of needs. In previous section, we described some task automation tools offering different composition paradigms. From their analysis it emerged that some tools (e.g., IFTTT) support the creation of rules by non-technical users but they show a low degree of customization; other tools (e.g., Node-RED) permit the creation of rules that fit very well the user needs but require technical skills. In order to find a trade-off between rule expressiveness and simplicity of the composition technique, we designed the 5W composition paradigm. The paradigm design took place by means of an elicitation study that involved 25 participants divided into 6 groups. The starting point of the elicitation study was the 5W model, typically adopted in journalism to analyze the complete story about a fact by answering to the 5 questions: (1) *Who* did it?; (2)*What* happened? (3) *When* did it take place?; (4) *Where* did it take place?; (5) *Why* did it happen?. The 5W model was adopted during the elicitation study to guide participants in proposing user interfaces and interaction techniques that support the creation of rules in term of events and actions defined by answering to the five questions. As result of the elicitation study, we obtained three different composition techniques that were implemented in three different systems. Such systems have been compared during a controlled experiment where further 40 participants were involved. During the experiment, we also introduced IFTTT as baseline. This experiment revealed that, in terms of user performances and user preferences, the composition paradigm reported in this paper outperforms the other two elicited paradigms and the one implemented in IFTTT. In this paper, we omitted details about the studies because they are already submitted for a publication [3]. Instead, this paper is more focused on the EFESTO technical aspects.

3.2 Extending EFESTO with the 5W Model: A Scenario

We now illustrate a usage scenario to help the reader to understand the 5W composition paradigm implemented in EFESTO. A user, Arya, wants to create a rule to automatically

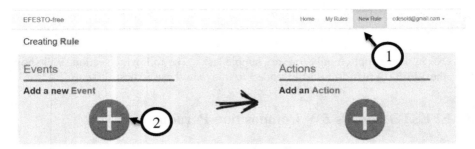

Fig. 1. EFESTO: the interface for rule creation. (Color figure online)

turn on her home heating and close roll-up the shutter in living room when her smart watch is near to her home or when the home temperature is below 22 °C. To create this rule, Arya starts by clicking the "New Rule" button in the navigation bar (Fig. 1, circle 1) and the "Creating Rule" interface appears (Fig. 1). EFESTO now shows the main area in which a rule is defined. The left side is for specifying the triggering events, and the right side is to define the actions to be activated by the selected services.

A wizard procedure, activated by the green "+" button highlighted by circle 2 in Fig. 1, guides Arya in defining the rule events in a full-automated fashion. The wizard sequentially shows some pop-up windows in which the service, its events and temporal and spatial conditions are specified. According to WYSIWYG approach, the wizard steps allow the user to define an event in terms of *Which* is the service to be monitored for detecting the triggering event (Fig. 2a), *What* service event has to be monitored (Fig. 2b), *When* and *Where* the event has to occur (Fig. 2c). The specification of *When* and *Where* conditions is optional. Following the wizard process, Arya selects the *Android Wear* object (Which) and the *Position changed* event (What). She also constraints the event triggering in the time interval 7.00 p.m. and 10.00 p.m. (When) and around her home address (Where). At the end of the wizard procedure, the event is defined and its summary appears under the "Events" area (Fig. 2d, circle 1).

After the event definition, Arya starts the creation of an action by clicking on the "Add an action" button in the Actions area (Fig. 2d). The button activates a wizard that helps the user define an action in terms of *Which* service will execute the action as a consequence of the event(s), *What* action the service has to perform and *When* and *Where* the action can be performed. In this scenario, Arya chooses the Heating (Which) and the "Open Rollup Shutter" as action to be activated (What), without specifying any spatial or temporal constraint.

In EFESTO, users may either define first all the events and then the actions, or define first a basic rule with one event and one action and then include new events and new actions. Events and actions can be added or removed at any time fostering a **dynamic modification of the running mashup**. Further events can be added by clicking one of the two green "+" buttons labeled And/Or (Fig. 2d, circle 2). When choosing the "And" button the definition of a new event starts that will cause the execution of the rule action(s) if all conditions of all events are satisfied. The "Or"

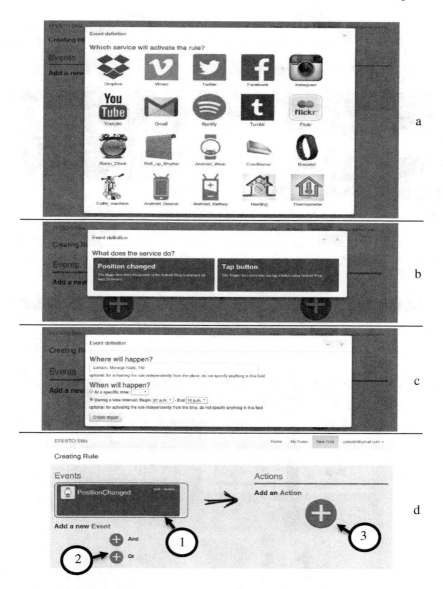

Fig. 2. EFESTO wizard procedure for event specification: (a) the wizard first asks to select the service that will activate the event; (b) as second step, the event is selected among those offered by the chosen service; (c) temporal and spatial constraints are defined; (d) the event has been defined and the user can define further events or actions. (Color figure online)

button determines the addition of a new event that will cause the execution of the rule action(s), if at least one event is triggered. Once the rule is created, it can be saved by entering a short description of the rule (the *Why* in the 5W model).

Fig. 3. Rule under creation during the rapid mashup challenge.

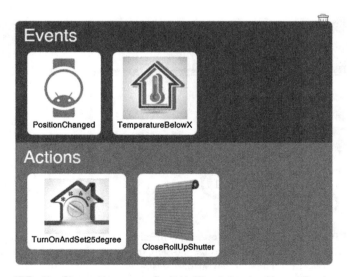

IF Position Changed happens on Android_ Wear in London, Monega Road 142 between 7 p.m. and 10 p.m. **OR** Temperature Below 22 happens on thermometer between 7 p.m. and 10 p.m.

THEN Turn On And Set25degree from heating **AND** Close Roll Up Shutter from Roll_up_ Shutter in Living Room

Fig. 4. Summary of the rule created during the rapid mashup challenge.

Coming back to the Arya scenario, she decides to enrich her rule by adding further events and actions. She continues by clicking the "OR" green plus button in the Events area (Fig. 2d, circle 2) to activate the wizard procedure to add a new event. She then selects the *Thermometer* object and chooses the *Temperature Below X* as event, also setting the same temporal constraints already defined for the Android Wear object.

Arya concludes the rule creation by adding another action in the rule: she clicks on the "Add an action" button in the Actions area (see Fig. 2d, circle 3). Following the wizard procedure, she selects the *Roll Up Shutter* object and the *Close Roll Up Shutter* action (see Fig. 3). Before saving the rule, Arya annotates it to indicate the rule purpose, i.e., "Automation of my home heating". After saving the rule, a window shows the summary of the rule with its details (Fig. 4).

4 EFESTO Implementation

4.1 Adopted Technologies

EFESTO is a Web application implemented with the Java Spring framework [28]. The User Interface (UI) was completely developed with Thymeleaf, a Java HTML5 template engine that substitutes the traditional JSP technology. Thymeleaf, in fact, makes the UI development faster, the code more compact and UI pages can be displayed in browsers without the need to deploy the Web application, also working as static prototypes. In addition, in order to obtain a professional UI look&feel, as well as UI responsiveness on different devices, we integrated the Bootstrap framework. The final system has been deployed on a virtual machine (4 core, 8 GB RAM, Windows Server 2012) instantiated in the Windows Azure cloud platform.

4.2 Architecture and Feature Checklist

The proposed task automation extension was designed starting from some modules already developed in the EFESTO mashup framework [4]. The new platform architecture presents a strong modularity, as shown in Fig. 5, thanks to the decoupling of the interaction layer from the other platform modules. The architecture design, in fact, was driven by the need to develop a general platform that can be easily customized by changing the composition paradigm implemented in the interaction layer [29], fostering its adoption in different domains and contexts.

The core part of the new architecture, depicted in Fig. 5, consists of a *Service Handler* and a *Rule Engine* module, which run on the remote Web server. The *Service Handler* provides a JSON abstract representation of Web Services and Smart Objects to the *Rule Generator*, which runs on Web browsers and is in charge of creating a visual representation of services and objects to the users. The *Rule Engine*, starting from the rule defined by the users with the EFESTO UI, **orchestrates the integration logic** of the involved services by instantiating a rule object representing a **logic mashup.** Such object is monitored by the Rule Engine every N minutes (3 min in our current implementation) to check events triggering and, in case, to activate consequent actions

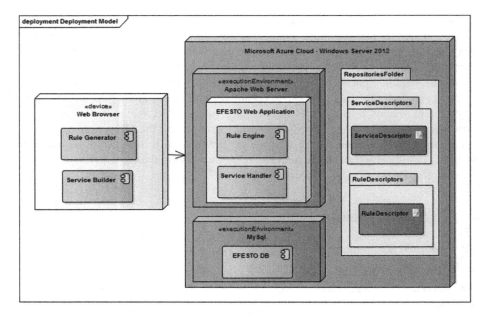

Fig. 5. The EFESTO extensions supporting the definition and execution of ECA rules for smart object synchronization.

(the **logic components**). The rule object is active on the platform even if the user is not logged-in, and until it is removed by the users (**Long-living Instantiation Lifecycle**).

EFESTO **run-time location** is on the **server**. The client is used as a front-end to allow the user to access the representation of services and synchronize them according to the 5W composition paradigm.

In its current version, EFESTO is used only for private and academic purposes. However, we aim at building a **public community** to promote the sharing of rules for smart space configurations.

4.3   Focus on the Rule Engine

In this section, we focus on the *Rule Engine,* which is the component supporting the new task automation features. An overview of its software organization is provided by the UML class diagram reported in Fig. 6. The core of this diagram is the **Rule** class that represents user-defined rules. A Rule object stores details about events and actions by using the lists *triggers* and *actions*, containing respectively objects instances of **Trigger** and **Action** classes. Such classes extend the **5WDetails** class that provides methods for setting trigger/action details according to the 5W model, i.e. *who, what, where* and *when.* For a trigger, *who* is the service name, *what* is the name of the trigger event, *where* is the place around which the event has to be triggered, *when* is the time interval/exact time when the event has to be triggered. For an action, *who* is the service name, *what* is the name of the action to invoke, *where* specifies a location of the service

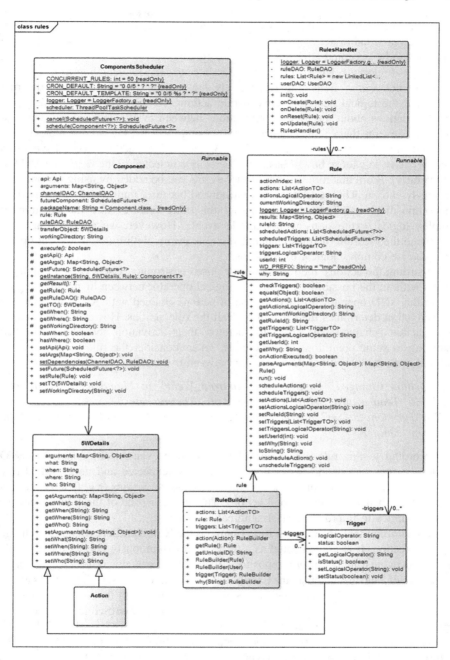

Fig. 6. UML class diagram of the rule creation components.

in case of multiple choices (e.g. in case of different air conditioners in a home, *where* specifies an air conditioner in a specific room), *when* indicates the exact time when the action has to be executed after the event(s) triggering.

Further important **Rule** class attributes are *triggersLogicalOperator* and *actionsLogicalOperator,* indicating respectively the logical operator between the rule events and the logical operator between rule actions. At the current state, we posed some restrictions about the logical connections between events and actions. The first one regards events that can be chained only by using the same logical operator. In fact, as described in the scenario reported in Sect. 3.2, when users add the second event to a rule, they have to choose how it has to be logically connected to the first one (AND or OR operator). From that moment on, further events can be added by using the operator previously chosen. This restriction was introduced because, until now, we focused on the composition paradigm, simplifying all the other features like the creation of complex logical expressions with multiple events. However, we already started to investigate the creation of rules chaining multiple events with different logical operators to create complex logical expressions.

Regarding the actions, the restriction we posed is stronger. Users can add multiple actions without the possibility to choose a logical operator between them, applying by default the AND operator. In fact, in case of actions chained with AND operator, the rule activation determines the execution of all the rule actions. However, supposing a set of actions chained with the OR operator, their activation should be specified according to some conditions. For example, let us consider the rule of the scenario reported in Sect. 3.2 with an OR operator between the actions:

IF "Position Changed" happens on "Android_Wear" in "London, Monega Road 142" OR "Temperature Below X" happens on "Thermometer"
THEN "Turn On And Set25degree" from "Heating" OR "Close Roll Up Shutter" from "Roll_up_ Shutter"

According to this rule, when one of the two rule events is triggered, EFESTO should activates one of the two actions. To avoid unexpected and uncontrolled rule behaviors, users should define some criteria to activate the actions (e.g. first try the first action and, if it fails, try the second action). This aspect is one of the future work we already planned to improve our task automation tool.

Another important object in the Rule Engine is the **RuleHandler,** which is in charge of rules creation. It is implemented as a thread that continuously checks for new rule descriptors in the *Rule Descriptor* repository. Every time a new rule is detected, it creates an instance of Rule that is sent to the **ComponentScheduler**. This scheduler stores a pool of rules exploiting the **ThreadPoolTaskScheduler** Spring class that natively supports the scheduling and execution of generic tasks. The **ComponentScheduler** execution logic is based on an event-driven, publish-subscribe paradigm since it establishes how the occurrence of published events cause the execution of subscribed operations [30, 31]. The **ComponentScheduler** supports two types of Web service events, i.e., the ones triggered by a service and immediately notified to a third party service (the ComponentScheduler in our case), and the ones triggered by a service that determines a state change in the service. In the first case, the ComponentScheduler, when notified by a service about a new triggered event, checks if all the other rule events are also triggered and, in case, executes the rule actions. In the second case, the scheduler checks every N minutes the rule events and, if triggered, executes the rule actions.

The rule creation process is summarized by the sequence diagram reported in Fig. 7. The process starts when the user, interacting with EFESTO for the creation of a rule (see Sect. 3.2), saves the rule. In that moment, the EFESTO CreationRulePage invokes the *generateRule()* method on the **RuleGenerator** class that translates the rule defined by the user into an XML descriptor (see Fig. 9). In parallel, the RuleHandler checks if new rules are stored in the *RuleDescriptors* Repository. When the new rule is detected, a **Rule** object is created and passed to the **ComponentScheduler** that starts to monitor its events.

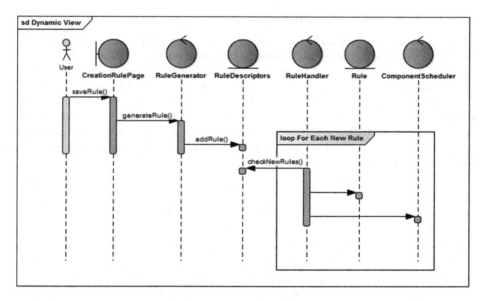

Fig. 7. Sequence diagram illustrating the interaction among the classes involved in the rule creation process.

4.4   Managing Temporal and Spatial Constraints

As already discussed in the previous sections, the interaction paradigm implemented in EFESTO is based on the 5W model to build rules coupling multiple events and conditions exposed by smart objects and web services, and for defining temporal and spatial constraints on rule activation and actions execution. In the following sub-sections, technical details about temporal and spatial constraints are reported.

4.4.1   Temporal Constraints
EFESTO allows the definition of temporal restrictions on rule events and actions. In case of events, it guides users in defining when (exact moment or time interval) an event must be triggered to activate the rule actions. In case of actions, it allows to

Table 1. Crono expression syntax details[a]

Name	Required	Allowed values	Allowed special characters
Seconds	Y	0–59	, - * /
Minutes	Y	0–59	, - * /
Hours	Y	0–23	, - * /
Day of month	Y	1–31	, - * ? / L W C
Month	Y	0–11 or JAN–DEC	, - * /
Day of week	Y	1–7 or SUN–SAT	, - * ? / L C #
Year	N	empty or 1970–2099	, - * /

[a]http://www.quartz-scheduler.org/documentation/quartz-2.x/tutorials/crontrigger.html

postpone the action execution in a specific moment or after a certain time. We exploited the *CronExpression* syntax to codify these temporal constraints in rule descriptors and check them in Rule Engine. A *cron* expression is a string consisting of six or seven subexpressions (fields) that describe individual details of the schedule. These fields, separated by white spaces, can contain any of the allowed values with various combinations of the allowed characters for that field. Table 1 shows the fields in the expected order while Table 2 reports some example of cron expressions and their means. In our platform, we used the *Quartz Job Scheduling Library* to integrate such expressions in rule descriptor [32].

Table 2. Crono expressions examples and their means[a]

Expression	Means
0 0 12 * * ?	Fire at 12:00 PM (noon) every day
0 0/5 14, 18 * * ?	Fire every 5 min starting at 2:00 PM and ending at 2:55 PM, AND fire every 5 min starting at 6:00 PM and ending at 6:55 PM, every day
0 0-5 14 * * ?	Fire every minute starting at 2:00 PM and ending at 2:05 PM, every day
0 15 10 ? * 6L	Fire at 10:15 AM on the last Friday of every month
0 15 10 ? * 6#3	Fire at 10:15 AM on the third Friday of every month

[a]https://docs.oracle.com/cd/E12058_01/doc/doc.1014/e12030/cron_expressions.htm

4.4.2 Spatial Constraints

EFESTO allows the definition of constraints on events triggers and action execution by specifying geographical addresses or place names. In particular, it supports two types of spatial constraints. Let us consider the following rules:

(R1) IF "Android Wear device" position changed and it is around "Monega Road 142, London" THEN "switch on home heating".

(R2) IF "air conditioner" in "living room" is "switched on" THEN "close roll up shutter" in "living room".

In R1, the spatial constraint on the *Android Wear device* event exploits the device GPS position while in R2 the spatial constraints on the *air conditioner* event and on the *roll up shutter* action are the room names. To assist users in defining the right spatial constraint, during the rule creation wizard, if the device exposes a specific GPS position like in rule R1, EFESTO asks users to type an address place which is converted in coordinates by using the Google Maps Geocoding API. On the contrary, if a group of same devices can be placed in different positions identified by a name like in R2, EFESTO shows a drop-down menu to choose a specific place. It is evident how these two types of spatial constraints are strictly related to the nature of the device. In the first case, the Android Wear has a GPS spatial position. In the second case, the devices (air conditioner and roll up shutter) are an abstraction of a more complex system, i.e., the domotic system, which integrates different devices of the same type that have different positions (air conditioner and roll up shutter installed in different rooms). EFESTO abstracts from these details, facilitating the end users in defining the spatial constraint depending on the nature of the device.

Another difference exists between spatial constraints defined on events and actions. In case of spatial constraints defined on events, every time the **ComponentScheduler** checks if the rule events are triggered, it also checks if the spatial constraints (as well as the time constraint) are satisfied. To do this, EFESTO invokes a method on the device to know its position. If the device returns its coordinates, EFESTO checks if they are around the point specified by the user rule (in the radius of 100 m; we are going to implement a feature to assist users in defining the radius). If the device returns a place name, EFESTO performs a syntactical comparison between the returned position name and the position name defined in the rule.

In case of spatial constraints defined on actions, every time the **ComponentScheduler** determines that rule events are triggered, it invokes an action of a service specifying the place name or coordinates. For example, in R2 there is the action *"close roll up shutter in living room"*. EFESTO invokes the methods *close roll up shutter* parametrized with the room name. In this example, we assumed that the domotic system exposes a method *close roll up shutter* with the *room name* parameter to close the right roll-up shutter. However, in real contexts, this scenario could be more complex due to a strong heterogeneity of method syntaxes, device protocols and service technologies. For these reasons, since until now the goal of our studies has been the design of a composition paradigm for the end users, we simplified these technical details. Anyway, we can safely assume that middleware like AT&T M2X[2] or Azure IoT Suite[3] can be used to mediate the access to different service technologies [33].

4.5 Rule and Service Descriptors

Service and Rule descriptors play an important role in the Rule Engine. A service descriptor is written by the platform administrator to register a new service. Such

---

[2] https://m2x.att.com.

[3] https://www.microsoft.com/en/server-cloud/internet-of-things/azure-iot-suite.aspx.

descriptors are codified according to a JSON grammar we defined. Such JSON grammar guarantees the registration of any (web, object) service in the platform, as long as it provides a RESTful API, thus allowing **hybrid mashups**. For example, an Android Wear device descriptor is reported in Fig. 8. It starts with a heading reporting two attributes, i.e., *name* and *url*. The first one is the service name while second one indicates the Web page documentation (if any). The third attribute, *body*, is a JSON object containing all the information to invoke service events and actions. In particular, the body object contains a set of attributes (*appId*, *appSecret*, *restUri*, *tokenUri*, *tokenExpiredCode*, and *authentication*) to build the methods invocation. The last body attribute is the *functions* array that lists different JSON objects expressing the events, actions, and general methods. In the example of Fig. 8, the first and second *function* objects describe events by using the attributes *type*, *name*, *path*, *method* and *response*. *Type* disambiguates the kind of function, i.e., event, action or method. *Name* reports the name of the function that is shown in the user interface. *Path* specifies the URI that has to be chained to the *restUri* attribute to invoke the specific service event. *Method* indicates the type of RESTful query, e.g., GET or POST. *Response* specifies the type of service response, e.g., JSON, XML, and HTML. The third *function* object represents an action by using the same attributes of an event. An optional attribute can be added in *event* or *action* objects, i.e., *param*, used to parametrize the RESTful query. For example, the descriptor of the *Thermometer* object (described in the Scenario reported in Sect. 3.2) has the event TemperatureBelowX that returns a Boolean results according to the temperature the user wants to monitor. The X value of this event represents the parameter set by users during the wizard process. Such value is used as parameter of the event method to query the Thermometer and to verify if the temperature is below a user-defined threshold. The fourth *function* object represents a method that the platform can invoke to get service data. For example, if a rule event has a geographical constraint, EFESTO can verify the service position by invoking a specific method, like the one reported in Fig. 8 (rows 34–39).

The rule descriptor is automatically generated by the RuleGenerator module during the wizard process. When the rule is saved, the RuleGenerator sends the final rule descriptor to the *Rule Descriptor* repository (see Fig. 5). As described in Sect. 4.3, the **RuleHandler** instantiates the rule object starting from this descriptor. The rule descriptor syntax was created according to our 5W model. In Fig. 9 an example of rule is reported. The descriptor header is characterized by the attributes *userId*, *ruleId*, *why*, *triggers_logical_opearator*, *actions_logical_opearator*. *userId* is the identification number the user had in the database; *ruleId* is the number that uniquely identifies the rule; *why* is the text the user typed to annotate the rule answering to the why question; *triggers_logical_opearator* specifies the logical operator the user choses to connect the events; *actions_logical_opearator* is the logical operator to connect the actions (always AND at the current status). After these attributes, there are two arrays, *events* and *actions*. In each array, there are JSON objects that describe events/actions in term of *who*, *what*, *what_parameter*, *when* and *when*. *who* is the name of the service, *how* is reported in the related service descriptor; *what* is the function (event or action) name *how* is reported in the related service descriptor; *what_parameter* is an optional

```
1  {
2    "name": "Android Wear",
3    "url": "https://www.myandroidwear.com/apidocs/en/api/v2"
4    "body": {
5      "appId": "VTnA9hAIsnGJ2OaiVv10KudZYwqL5Gjsf4s",
6      "appSecret": "Jokez2lH6hfnrXj6l7LgKa2A5Dtlksw5A4",
7      "restUri": "https://api.myandroidwear.com/",
8      "redirectUri": "https://localhost/callback/androidwear",
9      "tokenExpiredCode": 401,
10     "authentication": "OAuth1",
11     "functions": [
12       {
13         "type": "event",
14         "name": "Tap Button",
15         "path": "v2/tap Button/",
16         "method": "GET",
17         "response": "json"
18       },
19       {
20         "type": "event",
21         "name": "Position Changed",
22         "path": "v2/position_changed/",
23         "method": "GET",
24         "response": "json"
25       },
26       {
27         "type": "action",
28         "name": "SendANotification",
29         "path": "v2/send_notification/",
30         "method": "POST",
31         "response": "json"
32       },
33       {
34         "type": "method",
35         "name": "getPosition",
36         "path": "v2/getPosition/",
37         "method": "GET",
38         "response": "json",
39         "data_type": "coordinates"
40       }
41     ]
42   }
43 }
```

```
1  {
2    "userId" : 44,
3    "ruleId" : "25.json",
4    "why" : "Enjoy my Wakeup",
5    "triggers_logical_opearator": "OR",
6    "actions_logical_opearator": "AND"
7    "events" : [ {
8        "who" : "Android Wear",
9        "what" : "Position Changed",
10       "when" : "0 0/1 9 ? * ?",
11       "where" : "51.544411, 0.038814"
12     },
13     {
14       "who" : "Thermometer",
15       "what" : "Temperature Below X",
16       "what_parameter" : "22",
17       "when" : "0 0/1 9 ? * ?",
18       "where" : ""
19     }
20    ],
21    "actions" : [ {
22        "who" : "Roll-upShutter",
23        "what" : "Close",
24        "when" : "",
25        "where" : "bedroom"
26     },{
27       "who" : "Heating",
28       "what" : "TurnOnAndSet25Degree",
29       "when" : "",
30       "where" : ""
31     }
32    ]
33 }
```

Fig. 8. Example of an XML service descriptor related to an Android Wear device

Fig. 9. Example of an XML descriptor related to a rule

parameter that indicates the parameter to invoke the function; *when* reports the time constraint according to the cron syntax; *where* specifies the location (coordinates or location name).

5   EFESTO Level of Maturity

The current version of the EFESTO platform is the results of a 5-years research. During this period, we adopted a user-centred approach with the main goal of identifying how mashup composition paradigms could really help the users themselves. Our research is indeed strongly inspired by and oriented towards End-User Development principles [34]. The first version of EFESTO was a platform designed to enable end users to explore information by creating interactive workspaces [4]. Within a Web composition environment, end users dynamically create "live mashups" where relevant information, extracted from heterogeneous data sources - including the Linked Open Data [5] – is integrated according to visually defined queries. Visualizations of the resulting data sets can be flexibly shaped-up at runtime. Functions, exposed by local or remote services, also allow users to manipulate the resulting data depending on their situational needs.

The initial version of EFESTO, mainly devoted to the integration of data sources and the visualization of the resulting data sets, has been then extended in the light of the proliferation of smart objects that represent new sources of data and functionalities. The goal of the new extensions is to allow non-technical users to establish communications among smart objects, in order to program their behavior in a more powerful and meaningful way. The implementation of the current prototype still needs to be refined. We are however confident that the visual composition paradigm encounters the needs and capability of non-programmers, due to the user-centered approach that was adopted for its design. An elicitation study was indeed conducted to identify possible assess the usability of the visual paradigm for expressing composition rules. Different prototypes, implementing different the visual paradigms emerged from the study, were then compared during a controlled experiment. The results show that the composition paradigm presented in this paper increases the effectiveness, the efficiency and the satisfaction of both programmers and non-programmers also in comparison with well-known tools, such as IFTTT [3].

6   ICWE 2016 Rapid Mashup Challenge

During the Rapid Mashup Challenge, we illustrated the new composition paradigm implemented in EFESTO by showing the creation of a rule by means of a demo that followed the same flow of actions as the reference scenario described in Sect. 3. A video reproducing the demo is available at https://youtu.be/AosavGP657k.

Getting prepared for the challenge actually did not require additional efforts as the objects composed during the demo were already registered in the platform. We only made sure that their descriptors and the adapters for invoking them were running correctly. During the demo everything worked perfectly.

7   Conclusion

One key aspect in the future of the IoT will be to put in the hands of end users software tools offering natural and expressive paradigms to compose smart objects. Mashup paradigms can suit very well the need for synchronizing different objects to program the behavior of smart spaces. Adequate tools can enable non-expert users to achieve this goal. The work presented in this paper goes in this direction, as it concentrates on specializing a generic mashup platform for the composition of services that enable accessing/controlling smart things. The peculiarity of the presented platform is the composition paradigm: it was elicited and validated with the help of end users and then validated by means of controlled experiments. We are therefore very confident that this paradigm encounters the need and capabilities of non-expert programmers, letting them to take advantage of IoT technology.

Of course, there are still several aspects to be investigated. First of all, to further extend the capability of EFESTO in supporting the EUD of smart spaces, we are planning future work to understand if and how the addition and the initial configuration of new objects into smart environments could be performed by non-technical users. Actually, our current prototype requires the intervention of expert programmers to define JSON-based object descriptors. We would like to understand whether there can be simple procedures, also based on natural (e.g., gesture-based, proximity-based) interaction paradigms that could (at least partially) enable non-technical users to perform these activities. This implies the identification of a "component model", i.e., a set of conceptual elements abstracting the underlying technology, which can mediate between the technical features to be addressed to program smart objects (the components) and the interaction layer supporting the customization by end users of objects by means of high-level programming constructs.

We also aim to understand how, using recent digital printing technologies, the "fabrication" of smart objects (including the design and production of the physical objects, and the definition of their programming interfaces) can be conducted interactively with the support of visual EUD environments.

References

1. Atzori, L., Iera, A., Morabito, G.: The Internet of Things: a survey. Comput. Netw. **54**(15), 2787–2805 (2010)
2. Tetteroo, D., Markopoulos, P., Valtolina, S., Paternò, F., Pipek, V., Burnett, M.: End-user development in the Internet of Things era. In: Proceedings of CHI 2015, Seoul, pp. 2405–2408 (2015)
3. Desolda, G., Ardito, C., Matera, M.: Empowering end users to customize their smart environments: model, composition paradigms and tools. Technical report (2016)
4. Desolda, G., Ardito, C., Matera, M.: EFESTO: a platform for the end-user development of interactive workspaces for data exploration. In: Daniel, F., Pautasso, C. (eds.) RMC 2015. CCIS, vol. 591, pp. 63–81. Springer, Heidelberg (2016). doi:10.1007/978-3-319-28727-0_5
5. Desolda, G.: Enhancing workspace composition by exploiting linked open data as a polymorphic data source. In: Damiani, E., Howlett, R.J., Jain, L.C., Gallo, L., De Pietro, G. (eds.) Intelligent Interactive Multimedia Systems and Services. SIST, vol. 40, pp. 97–108. Springer, Heidelberg (2015). doi:10.1007/978-3-319-19830-9_9
6. Daniel, F., Matera, M.: Mashups: Concepts, Models and Architectures. Springer, Heidelberg (2014)
7. Coronado, M., Iglesias, C.A.: Task automation services: automation for the masses. IEEE Internet Comput. **20**(1), 52–58 (2016)
8. IFTTT. https://ifttt.com/. Accessed 3 Dec 2015
9. Ardito, C., Costabile, M.F., Desolda, G., Lanzilotti, R., Matera, M., Picozzi, M.: Visual composition of data sources by end-users. In: Proceedings of AVI 2014, Como, 28–30 May, pp. 257–260 (2014)

10. ELASTIC.IO GMBH. http://www.elastic.io/. Accessed 25 July 2016
11. Zapier. https://zapier.com/. Accessed 25 Mar 2016
12. Atooma. https://www.atooma.com/. Accessed 25 Mar 2016
13. Cabitza, F., Fogli, D., Lanzilotti, R., Piccinno, A.: Rule-based tools for the configuration of ambient intelligence systems: a comparative user study. Multimed. Tools Appl. **75**(248), 1–21 (2016)
14. AutomateIt. http://automateitapp.com/. Accessed 25 Mar 2016
15. Tasker. http://tasker.dinglisch.net/index.html. Accessed 25 Mar 2016
16. Technology IE. http://nodered.org/. Accessed 26 Nov 2015
17. Namoun, A., Nestler, T., Angeli, A.: Conceptual and Usability Issues in the Composable Web of Software Services. In: Daniel, F., Facca, F.M. (eds.) ICWE 2010. LNCS, vol. 6385, pp. 396–407. Springer, Heidelberg (2010). doi:10.1007/978-3-642-16985-4_35
18. Namoun, A., Nestler, T., Angeli, A.D.: Service composition for non-programmers: prospects, problems, and design recommendations. In: Proceedings of ECOWS 2010. Washington, DC, pp. 123–130 (2010)
19. Zang, N., Rosson, M.B.: What's in a mashup? And why? Studying the perceptions of web-active end users. In: Proceedings of VL-HCC 2008, Herrsching, 15–19 September, pp. 31–38 (2008)
20. Bip.io. https://bip.io/. Accessed 25 Mar 2016
21. Spacebrew. http://docs.spacebrew.cc/. Accessed 25 Mar 2016
22. Zipato. https://www.zipato.com/. Accessed 25 March 2016
23. Fogli, D., Lanzilotti, R., Piccinno, A.: End-User development tools for the smart home: a systematic literature review. In: Streitz, N., Markopoulos, P. (eds.) DAPI 2016. LNCS, vol. 9749, pp. 69–79. Springer, Heidelberg (2016). doi:10.1007/978-3-319-39862-4_7
24. Wajid, U., Namoun, A., Mehandjiev, N.: Alternative representations for end user composition of service-based systems. In: Costabile, M.F., Dittrich, Y., Fischer, G., Piccinno, A. (eds.) IS-EUD 2011. LNCS, vol. 6654, pp. 53–66. Springer, Heidelberg (2011). doi:10.1007/978-3-642-21530-8_6
25. Namoun, A., Wajid, U., Mehandjiev, N.: Service composition for everyone: a study of risks and benefits. In: Dan, A., Gittler, F., Toumani, F. (eds.) ICSOC/ServiceWave -2009. LNCS, vol. 6275, pp. 550–559. Springer, Heidelberg (2010). doi:10.1007/978-3-642-16132-2_52
26. Barricelli, B.R., Valtolina, S.: Designing for end-user development in the Internet of Things. In: Díaz, P., Pipek, V., Ardito, C., Jensen, C., Aedo, I., Boden, A. (eds.) IS-EUD 2015. LNCS, vol. 9083, pp. 9–24. Springer, Heidelberg (2015). doi:10.1007/978-3-319-18425-8_2
27. Rode, J.A., Toye, E.F., Blackwell, A.F.: The fuzzy felt ethnography—understanding the programming patterns of domestic appliances. Pers. Ubiquitous Comput. **8**(3–4), 161–176 (2004)
28. Pivotal Software. https://spring.io/. Accessed 21 July
29. Ardito, C., Costabile, M.F., Desolda, G., Lanzilotti, R., Matera, M., Piccinno, A., Picozzi, M.: User-driven visual composition of service-based interactive spaces. J. Vis. Lang. Comput. **25**(4), 278–296 (2014)
30. Yu, J., Benatallah, B., Saint-Paul, R., Casati, F., Daniel, F., Matera, M.: A framework for rapid integration of presentation components. In: Proceedings of WWW 2007, Banff, 8–12 May, pp. 923–932 (2007)
31. Cappiello, C., Matera, M., Picozzi, M., Sprega, G., Barbagallo, D., Francalanci, C.: DashMash: a mashup environment for end user development. In: Auer, S., Díaz, O., Papadopoulos, G.A. (eds.) ICWE 2011. LNCS, vol. 6757, pp. 152–166. Springer, Heidelberg (2011). doi:10.1007/978-3-642-22233-7_11

32. Terracotta. http://www.quartz-scheduler.org/. Accessed 21 July
33. Li, S., Xu, L., Zhao, S.: The Internet of Things: a survey. Inf. Syst. Front. **17**(2), 243–259 (2015)
34. Costabile, M.F., Fogli, D., Mussio, P., Piccinno, A.: Visual interactive systems for end-user development: a model-based design methodology. IEEE Trans. Syst. Man Cybern. Part A Syst. Hum. **37**(6), 1029–1046 (2007)

Toolet: An Editor for Web-Based Tool Appropriation by Hobby Programmers

Jeremías P. Contell[✉] and Oscar Díaz

ONEKIN Web Engineering Group,
University of the Basque Country (UPV/EHU), San Sebastián, Spain
{jeremias.perez,oscar.diaz}@ehu.eus

Abstract. Web appropriation implies adapting a web application to the user's practice in ways that might not be conceived by the application designers. This might need to be conducted by the application's users themselves. This requires for appropriation to be described at an adequate level of abstraction. This paper explores first steps in using Query By Example as a way to denote the semantics of situational, idiosyncratic operations. We explore this approach through *Toolet*, an editor for Web tool appropriation built on top of Google Sheets.

Keywords: Web appropriation · Query By Example · Web augmentation

1 Context and Goals

Technology appropriation is being defined as "the process through which users adopt, adapt, and then incorporate a system with their practices" [4]. This process takes place in both the physical and the virtual world, but it is specially interesting for Web applications. Rationales are twofold. First, opportunity: the Web is becoming the place where an increasing number of applications are being migrated and hence, where users undertake a larger number of their daily activities. It might then be expected that numerous opportunities will emerge for adapting Web applications to the users' practices. Second, possibility: Web rendering is "malleable", i.e. client-side code can be transcoded at the browser using augmentation approaches [2]. In addition, two additional practices are paving the way forward: APIs and semantic annotations. APIs account for a programatic way to access complementary functionality that might not be available (or not in the desired way) in the Web counterpart. On the other side, semantic annotations facilitate the understanding and the hackability of the client-side code. This opens an opportunity for Web appropriation.

But this is not enough. Malleability might make Web appropriation possible but not affordable. And the problem is that appropriation is highly idiosyncratic. Unlike Web personalization (thought by designers), Web appropriation should be mostly conducted by the applications' users themselves. Indeed, appropriation implies adapting a system to the user's practices in ways they might not be even conceived by designers [3,11]. Hence, we see a challenge in describing

© Springer International Publishing AG 2017
F. Daniel and M. Gaedke (Eds.): RMC 2016, CCIS 696, pp. 94–107, 2017.
DOI: 10.1007/978-3-319-53174-8_6

Web appropriation on an adequate level of abstraction. The answer very much depends on both the kind of Web application and the target audience. We focus on *Web tools* and *hobby programmers*. By *Web tools* it is meant Web applications that support the manipulation of artifacts through the Web. Examples of Web tools include *Google Docs* or editors for different sorts of artifacts (e.g. mind maps[1], to-do lists[2], etc.). As for *hobby programmers*, they are defined as those spending ten or more hours a month programming, but they are not paid primarily to be a programmer [1]. This implies the programming effort to fit this ten-hour frame. Unfortunately, if appropriation of Web tools is conducted in terms of raw JavaScript, these ten hours will fall short. Raising the abstraction level and providing tool support is a possible way ahead. We explore this way through *"Toolet"*, an editor for Web tool appropriation built on top of Google Sheets.

Next sections describe work-in-progress with the help of an example: the appropriation of *MindMeister*. The remainder of the paper is structured as follows: Sect. 2 introduces the appropriation scenario that will be used to illustrate our approach. In Sect. 3 we describe our approach through a prototypical implementation. After that, in Sect. 4 we describe the level of maturity of our work and categorize the mashup tool and the generated mashup and in Sect. 5 we summarize the related work. Finally, Sect. 6 summarizes the conclusions and findings.

2 An Appropriation Scenario

MindMeister is a popular mind-map drawing tool. *MindMeister* is thought for schema drawing and brain storming. At the ONEKIN group, we use intensively *MindMeister* for brain storming but also for conducting PhD projects along Design Science guidelines [7]. This approach guides research projects through different milestones: define the setting, explicate the problem's cause, analyze the problem's consequences, etc. Students can add new nodes to their maps as they get acquainted about the different issues. This is the intended use of mind maps in general, and *MindMeister* in particular. However, quite often map nodes do not come from our own insights but from reading somewhere else's articles. Here, map nodes might not originate while drawing the mind map (at *MindMeister*) but when reading articles (e.g. at *Mendeley*[3]). This leads to our main premise:

> *Node creation at places other than the map editor might not be anticipated by MindMeister designers but it turns out of importance to our way of working.*

What we wanted was the possibility to create nodes for *MindMeister* maps but at places other than *MindMeister* (e.g. *Mendeley*). Specifically, we wanted to

---

[1] https://www.mindmeister.com/.

[2] https://www.rememberthemilk.com.

[3] https://www.mendeley.com/.

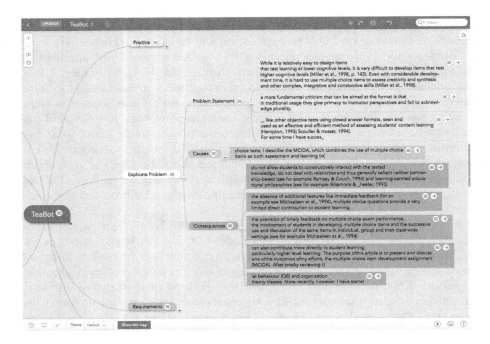

Fig. 1. *A* MindMeister *map: colored leaf nodes are obtained out of* Mendeley-*stored document highlighted quotes.*

highlight problems, causes and consequences when reading articles in Mendeley, and eventually, move to the *MindMeister* map, and find the highlighted quotes as nodes hanging from the right places in the map, i.e. the *Problem Statement* node, the *Causes* node or the *Consequences* node (see Fig. 1). The relationship between a quote and what this quote stands for (i.e. a cause, a consequence, etc.) is set in terms of colors: e.g. a quote in green accounts for the concept node with green background. Next Section addresses how this scenario can be described in *Toolet*.

3   *Toolet* at Work

Toolet is an editor to generate *toolet scripts*, i.e., browser extensions that augment Web tools with idiosyncratic operations, i.e. for Web tool appropriation. The *Toolet* editor (hereafter, just *Toolet*) conceives the Web as a database where each data source represents a table. *Toolet* is built on top of Google Sheets (see Fig. 2). Rather than facing the different ways data can be represented, we strive to hide this heterogeneity through a common tabular representation. Thus, *Toolet* abstracts Web tools in terms of *tables* while *toolet scripts* (hereafter, just *toolets*) are abstracted in terms of operations upon those tables. That is, *toolets* introduce new operations whose operational semantics is defined in terms of table

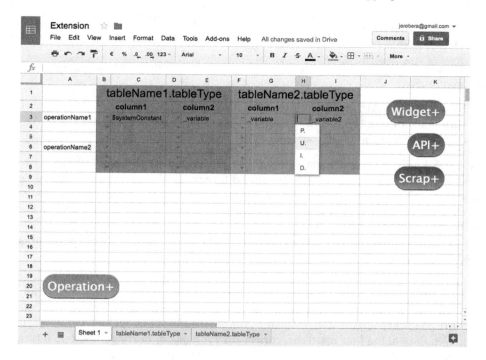

Fig. 2. Toolet *main window. Tables are created by pushing the right-side buttons, e.g..* Widget+ *for creating* Widget *tables. Tables include a signature and a type. Signatures are held in the main sheet (e.g.* Sheet 1*) whereas each table body is kept into a separated companion sheet (*tableName1.tableType*). Once tables are created, operations are described as QBE expressions. Button* Operation+ *assists during operation definition.*

manipulations using a Query-By-Example approach [16]. Back to the example, both *MindMeister* and *Mendeley* are abstracted in terms of tables. The *toolet* script will consult the *Mendeley* table and appropriately, update the *MindMeister* table, e.g. at the time *MindMeister* is loaded. Which columns are held by these tables depends on the example at hand. How these columns are obtained depends on the underlying mechanism used to obtain the data: scrapping, API calls or user interaction. Next subsections introduce the details.

3.1   Table Definition

Table definition involves both a table signature and a table body. The signature includes the table's name, the table's type and the columns. Table names are automatically obtained along the pattern *origin.type*, e.g. *mendeley.API*. As for the type, it can be

- *"API"*, for tables whose columns are obtained through API calls,
- *"Scrap"*, for tables whose columns are obtained by scrapping the HTML code,

– *"Widget"*, for tables whose columns stand for the input/output parameters of widgets components.

Next, the table body. It holds how columns are obtained depending on their type, namely,

– by annotating API documentation for API tables,
– through scraping the tool to be appropriated for Scrap tables,
– on the basis of the input/output parameters for Widget tables.

A table body is then a code snippet. As illustrated in the next sections, we strive for this code snippet to be generated for the most part. *Toolet* will bundle the code snippets for the different tables, and produce the corresponding *toolet script*, i.e. a Chrome plug-in that augments the Web tool at hand with the idiosyncratic behaviour.

Next, we illustrate the different table-creation modes through a running example. The resulting *toolet* is depicted in Fig. 7.

API Tables. API tables are obtained from API calls. Click on the *API+* button for a new browser tap to come up ("the Annotator tab"). From now on, visited pages are augmented with this *Annotator* tab, i.e. a widget for annotating Web data along four main categories: *HTTP request, query parameter, return parameter,* and *URL parameter*. The aim: recovering information that permits to populate an API table. In our example, we would like to obtain quotes (i.e. paragraph highlighted during reading) from articles held in a given *Mendeley* folder. No single *Mendeley* method provides that. Rather, a chain of method calls is needed. To obtain such chain, the user first collects information about those methods through the annotator. Second, a pipe-like approach serves to link one method's output parameter with another method's input parameter. Figure 3 provides an example. Users browse along *Mendeley's* Web pages that contain API documentation. When they find the methods of interest, annotator buttons are used to annotate the method call and the method parameters. Just highlight the text of interest, and push the appropriate button to indicate this text stands for an HTTP method, a Method URL, a URL parameter, etc. Resulting annotations appear in the *Annotator* tab (right-hand side). Parameter displays hold anchors from which pipelines can be set. In the example, folder method output ID serves to feed the documents method input ID parameter that stands for the document identifier. Parameters not participating in any pipe become the table's columns. This is the case of three parameter: *name, text* and *color*.

Once the annotator tab is closed, *Toolet* goes back to the Google Sheets where the API table is created. At this time, users can change column names at wish. Figure 7 shows the output for the *mendeley.API* table. For understandability sake, the user changed column names *name* and *text* for *folderName* and *quote*, respectively. But this is not enough. So far, we obtained the quotes for the *Mendeley* folder's documents. This quotes will become map nodes. But we need to know from where to hang these nodes, i.e. their parent nodes. This is obtained

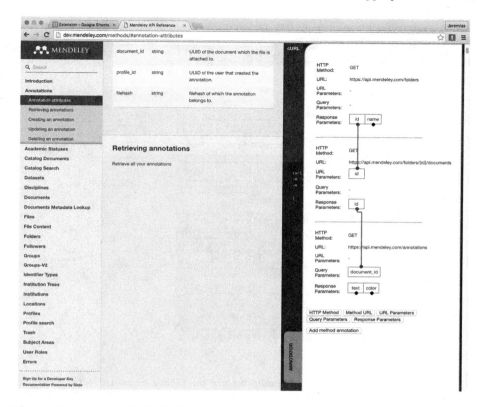

Fig. 3. Annotator *tab. Highlight text on the Web page, and push the appropriate button to indicate this text stands for an HTTP method, a Method URL, a URL parameter, etc. Annotations are shown at the top of the* Annotator *tab. Parameter displays hold anchors from which pipelines can be set. In the example, folder method output ID serves to feed the documents method input ID parameter that stands for the document identifier.*

through color matching: quotes become children of color-like nodes. We obtain nodes' colors through the *MindMeister* API. Following a process similar to the *mendeley.API*, the *mindmeister.API* table is created with five columns: *map_id, idea_id, parent_id, title* and *background_color*.

Scrap Tables. Scrap tables are obtained from the Web page of the tool to be appropriated. Click on the *Scrap+* button for being prompted for the tool's URL (e.g. www.mindmeister.com). This page is now augmented with a *XPath-finder* tab so that hovering around the page will highlight different HTML fragments. Click on the content of interest for *Toolet* to obtain the XPath expression. Keep clicking till *Toolet* infer an XPath expression that select all HTML nodes of interest. The *XPath-finder* tab will show an HTML representative of the elements being selected. Now, the user can select which fragment properties will become table columns while

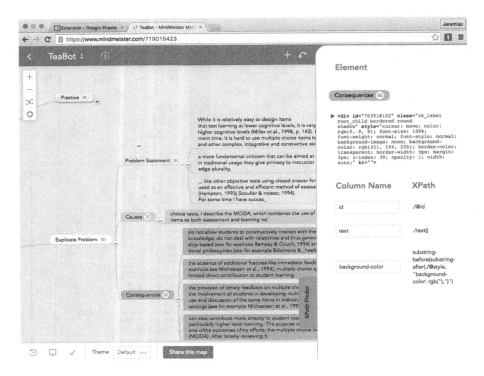

Fig. 4. *XPath Finder* tab. *Scrapped data become the table's columns. In the example, the ID, content and background color of the nodes are the data needed to conduct the appropriation.*

Toolet infers the XPath counterpart. Figure 4 shows the case for three properties: *id, text* and *background-color.* Close the tab to return to Google Sheets. Columns are re-named as *nodeID, nodeContent* and *backgroundColor.*

Widget Tables. In QBE, joins are denoted by using the same variable in two different columns (see later). This requires the two columns to pertain to the same type, i.e. range over the same set of values. When this is not the case, a mismatch occurs. As an example, our approach rests on shading *MindMeister* nodes with background colors taken from *Mendeley* so that the mapping between quotes (in *Mendeley*) and parent nodes (in *MindMeister*) can be set. Unfortunately, background colors in *Mendeley* are not those of *MindMeister*.

Overcoming data mismatches is not easy [14]. Service composition is an area that has extensively looked into this issue [9]. These techniques can be of interest here. Specifically, we are interested in those techniques that might require some augmentation of the Web page. For instance, the previous mismatch can be solved by extending the range of colors in *MindMeister* with those of *Mendeley's.* This requires to augment *Mendeley's* Web page. Widgets are the way to achieve it.

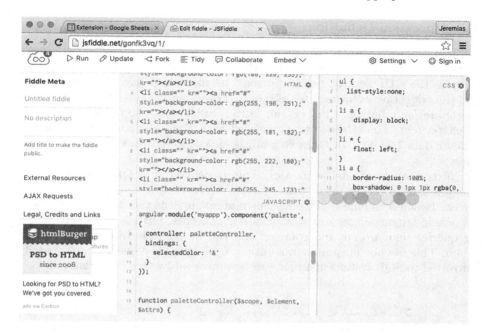

Fig. 5. JSFiddle *is used for widget creation. Symbols '&' and '@' denote input and output parameters. In the example, the* Palette *widget holds only an output parameter:* selectedColor. *These parameters will become the columns of the Widget table counterpart.*

By clicking on the *Widget+* button, developers are moved to *jsFiddle*[4]. Widget are now developed using *AngularJS* component notation[5]. These components have a well defined public-API for specifying both inputs and outputs. These parameters are specified in the configuration object used to create the new component. Figure 5 depicts the widget for our sample case. Its output parameter is *selectedColor* (lines 9–11). Inputs and outputs become columns of the Widget table counterpart. Think of widgets as layers on top of Web pages where their data is not obtained through scrapping but directly obtained from the code definition. For our running example, Fig. 7 depicts the *palette.WIDGET* table with its unique column: *selectedColor*.

---

[4] *jsFiddle* is a web application allowing users to create and execute code written in JavaScript, HTML, and CSS. It acts as a sandbox to easily check out your code without the need to install the corresponding frameworks. More information at https://jsfiddle.net.

[5] https://docs.angularjs.org/guide/component.

3.2   Operation Definition

An operation is a triplet: <*name, operationalSemantics, enactor*>. Let's start by the enactor. The enactor refers to the means to trigger the operation. This includes the GUI element (e.g. a button), its placement (e.g. the page footer) and the triggering event (e.g. on clicking). This description is achieved through the *Operation+* button. Click on this button to be moved to the Web tool (e.g. *MindMeister*). *MindMeister* is augmented with a panel that prompts for the enactor data (see Fig. 6). Once this tab is closed, we go back to *Toolet's* main view.

Next, the operational semantics. This is defined *à la* QBE, a GUI-based query language where users write queries by creating *example tables* on the screen. Benefits include that user needs minimal information to get started and the whole language contains relatively few concepts. QBE is especially suited for queries that are not too complex and can be expressed in terms of a few tables. This fits our purposes. In addition, QBE graphical queries can be easily converted to SQL statements, ready to be processed by the *Toolet* engine.

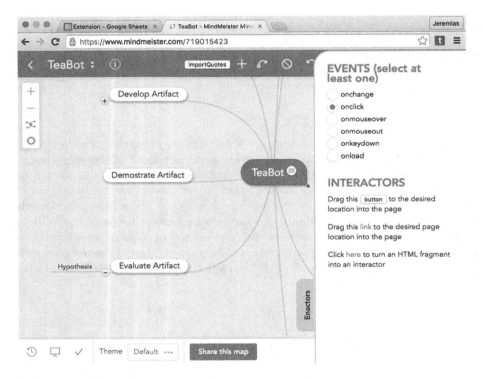

Fig. 6. *Enactor* tab: event definition, interactor definition and interactor placement are conducted through this tab during operation description. Note the new button "importQuotes" at the tool bar.

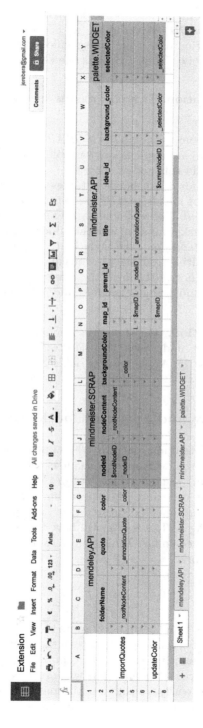

Fig. 7. *Operational semantics definition in* Toolet *showing the QBE queries for* importQuotes *and* updateColor.

In QBE, data needs and data updates are denoted by filling cells with system constants (e.g. *$rootNodeID*) or variables (e.g. *_nodeID*). Selection, insertion, deletion, and modification of a tuple are specified through the commands *P.*, *I.*, *D.*, and *U.*, respectively. Figure 7 depicts the case for *importQuotes* and *updateColor*.

The *importQuotes* operation. This operation is specified with the help of three rows (3–5):

1. the first row selects from *mindmeister.SCRAP* the *nodeContent* from the root node (kept in an application variable *$rootNodeID*). Variable *_rootNodeContent* will hold this node's content,
2. the second row accounts for a join between tables *mendeley.API* and *mindmeister.SCRAP*. Tuples of *mendeley.API* are constrained for its *folderName* to be the *_rootNodeContent*. The join commands for the color of the quote in *Mendeley* to match the background color of the node in *MindMeister* (*_color*). The quote (*_annotationQuote*) and the node ID (*_nodeID*) are selected,
3. finally, for each tuple resulting from the previous query, a tuple is inserted into table *mindmeister.API* (notice the *I.* in the margin). This tuple stands for a node whose *parent_id* and *title* are *_nodeId* and *_annotationQuote*, respectively.

The *updateColor* operation. This operation involves to update the *background_color* of the current node with the *selectedColor* obtained from the *palette.WIDGET* table (row 7). Application variable *$currentNodeID* holds the current node.

4   Level of Maturity and Feature Checklist

Toolet realizes an appropriation approach to Web applications. The tool is still under development. So far, the development includes the assistance tabs which are responsible for generating the different tables in Google Sheets. So obtained spreadsheet is next used as the canvas for specifying the new functionality in terms of a QBE query. At run time, a dedicated query engine will map this QBE query into the corresponding API calls. We still have to develop this engine. No evaluation has been conducted so far. Table 1 outlines *Toolet* features along the mashup conceptual framework.

5   Related Work

The spreadsheet paradigm is popular among mashup tools. The two main assumptions are (i) the possibility of organizing the representation of service composition in a two-dimensional space and (ii), the wide acceptance of spreadsheets among users [12]. The target audience is then end users who are already familiarized with spreadsheets, and hence, can easily transition to the mashup realm. Sharing a similar paradigm, *Toolet* exhibits main differences with these tools.

Table 1. Mashup and Mashup Tool feature checklist.

Mashup Feature Checklist

Mashup Type	Hybrid
Component Types	Data components
	Logic components
	UI components
Runtime Location	Client-side
Integration Logic	Orchestrated integration
Instantiation Lifecycle	Long-living

Mashup Tool Feature Checklist

Targeted End-User	Expert programmers
Automation Degree	Semi-automation
Liveness Level	Level 2
Interaction Technique	Spreadsheets
	Form-based
	Visual Language (Wiring, Explicit Control Flow)
Online User Community	None

Target audience. Most mashup tools target users with no programming skills. By contrast, *Toolet* requires technical skills.

Purpose. Broadly, mashup tools are used to create applications by composing third-party data. *Toolet* does not create a brand-new application but adapts an existing one.

Data Model. Mashup tools vary in the data model, i.e. the way in which they represent complex data in a cell-based layout. While *Mashroom* resorts to a nested table metaphor [15], [5] opt for using an XML-based data model. Similarly to [10], *Toolet* flattens complex data into atomic expressions that can be represented in cells.

Service invocation and composition. Most mashup tools resort to spreadsheet formulas to retrieve external data. Service composition is hidden with the formula. By contrast, *Toolet* tables main purpose is to specify service composition using a QBE approach. The challenge is not so much the invocation but the orchestration of different services in a declarative way. At this respect, *UQBE* [13] and *MashQL* [6] are two interesting exceptions. *UQBE* infers possible mappings between different sources and lets users interactively refine the results at query time. Since *UQBE* is targeted to non-programmers, it frees users from the complexities of service parameter mapping. Conversely, *Toolet* is intended to hobbyist programmers, and therefore, the parameter mapping is up to the user. As for *MashQL*, is a query language to mash up and fuse Linked-Data sources on the Web. Web data sources are seen as tables, and mashups as queries over these sources. Using a pipe metaphor, users define *MashQL* queries that will be automatically translated into and executed as SPARQL queries. *Toolet* focuses on Open APIs, no matter the data format, and the integration goes beyond data integration to consider the inlaying of the new functionality in the appropriated tool.

Runtime environment. Most mashup tools use the spreadsheet platform for both development and enactment. That is, the spreadsheet *is* the mashup application. Nevertheless, there are some exceptions such as *DataSheets* [8], a spreadsheet-based data-flow language that is integrated in a process composition platform. Once the data-flow is defined using a spreadsheet-like interface, the system translates it into BPEL code which is deployed and executed by a 3rd party BPEL engine. Similarly, *Toolet* uses spreadsheets for definition purposes, i.e. to obtain a *toolet* script. A *toolet* is realized as a browser plug-in that adapts a given Web tool to the practices of a given user group.

6   Conclusions

We described the early stages of *Toolet*, a browser extension for Google Chrome for helping users to adapt Web tools to their own practices. The aim is to hide complexity through a common table view. No matter how data is obtained (through APIs, Web Scrapping or user interactions), it is all represented as table columns. Next, new operations, better said, the operational semantics of these operations is specified using QBE.

An important concern of this approach is adaptive maintenance. Upgrades in either APIs or the tool's Web might break the *toolet* script apart. The risk is even higher than for traditional mashup applications. Since our approach to Web appropriation rests on scraping the tool's web and not only on API consultation (as most of mashup applications do), this makes *toolet* scripts more vulnerable. This spur even more the interest in coming up with declarative approaches that not only low the learning bar but also facilitate maintenance. Nevertheless, we believe there will be an increasing pressure to Web appropriation. The large list of feature requests that queue up in the tools' Web sites seems to suggest so. *MindMeister* is a case in point. The features requested accounts for hundreds!![6] We wonder how many of these petitions could be self-satisfied if suitable tools were available. *Toolet* attempts to provide some first insights.

Acknowledgment. Contell has a doctoral grant from the University of the Basque Country.

---

[6] https://support.mindmeister.com/hc/en-us/community/topics/200108207-MindMeister-Feature-Requests.

References

1. Hobbyist programmers: Don't call us hobbyists (by phil johnson). http://www. itworld.com/article/2702038/application-management/hobbyist-programmers-- don-t-call-us-hobbyists.html. Accessed 27 July 2016
2. Díaz, O., Arellano, C.: The augmented web: Rationales, opportunities, and challenges on browser-side transcoding. ACM Trans. Web **9**(2), 8:1–8:30 (2015)
3. Dix, A.: Designing for appropriation. In: Proceedings of the 21st British HCI Group Annual Conference on People and Computers: HCI... but not as we know it, vol. 2, pp. 27–30. British Computer Society (2007)
4. Fidock, J., Carroll, J.: Why do users employ the same system in so many different ways? IEEE Intell. Syst. **26**(4), 32–39 (2011)
5. Hoang, D.D., Paik, H.-Y., Ngu, A.H.H.: Spreadsheet as a generic purpose mashup development environment. In: Maglio, P.P., Weske, M., Yang, J., Fantinato, M. (eds.) ICSOC 2010. LNCS, vol. 6470, pp. 273–287. Springer, Heidelberg (2010). doi:10.1007/978-3-642-17358-5_19
6. Jarrar, M., Dikaiakos, M.D.A.: Data mashup language for the data web. In: LDOW, Citeseer (2009)
7. Johannesson, P., Perjons, E.: An Introduction to Design Science. Springer International Publishing, Cham (2014)
8. Lagares Lemos, A., Chai Barukh, M., Benatallah, B.: DataSheets: a spreadsheet-based data-flow language. In: Basu, S., Pautasso, C., Zhang, L., Fu, X. (eds.) ICSOC 2013. LNCS, vol. 8274, pp. 616–623. Springer, Heidelberg (2013). doi:10. 1007/978-3-642-45005-1_53
9. Li, X., Fan, Y., Jiang, F.: A classification of service composition mismatches to support service mediation. In: Sixth International Conference on Grid and Cooperative Computing (GCC 2007), pp. 315–321. IEEE (2007)
10. Obrenović, Ž., Gašević, D.: End-user service computing: spreadsheets as a service composition tool. IEEE Trans. Serv. Comput. **1**(4), 229–242 (2008)
11. Quinones, P.-A., Teasley, S.D., Lonn, S.: Appropriation by unanticipated users: looking beyond design intent and expected use. In: Proceedings of the 2013 Conference on Computer Supported Cooperative Work, pp. 1515–1526. ACM (2013)
12. Skrobo, D.: A Spreadsheet for End-User Service Composition. Ph.D. thesis, Ph. D. Dissertation. University of Zagreb (2007)
13. Tatemura, J., Chen, S., Liao, F., Po, O., Candan, K.S., Agrawal, D.: UQBE: uncertain query by example for web service mashup. In: Proceedings of the 2008 ACM SIGMOD International Conference on Management of Data, pp. 1275–1280. ACM (2008)
14. Velasco-Elizondo, P., Dwivedi, V., Garlan, D., Schmerl, B., Fernandes, J.M.: Resolving data mismatches in end-user compositions. In: Dittrich, Y., Burnett, M., Mørch, A., Redmiles, D. (eds.) IS-EUD 2013. LNCS, vol. 7897, pp. 120–136. Springer, Heidelberg (2013). doi:10.1007/978-3-642-38706-7_10
15. Wang, G., Yang, S., Han, Y.: Mashroom: end-user mashup programming using nested tables. In: Proceedings of the 18th International Conference on World Wide Web, ACM, pp. 861–870 (2009)
16. Zloof, M.M.: Query by example. In: Proceedings of the National Computer Conference and Exposition, pp. 431–438. ACM, 19–22 May 1975

On the Role of Context in the Design of Mobile Mashups

Valerio Cassani, Stefano Gianelli, Maristella Matera[(✉)], Riccardo Medana,
Elisa Quintarelli, Letizia Tanca, and Vittorio Zaccaria

Politecnico di Milano, Dipartimento di Elettronica,
Informazione e Bioingegneria, Milan, Italy
{valerio.cassani,stefano.gianelli}@mail.polimi.it,
{maristella.matera,riccardo.medana,elisa.quintarelli,
letizia.tanca,vittorio.zaccaria}@polimi.it

Abstract. This paper presents a design methodology and an accompanying platform for the design and fast development of Context-Aware Mobile mashUpS (CAMUS). The approach is characterized by the role given to context as a first-class modeling dimension used to support *(i)* the identification of the most adequate resources that can satisfy the users' situational needs and *(ii)* the consequent tailoring at runtime of the provided data and functions. Context-based abstractions are exploited to generate models specifying how data returned by the selected services have to be merged and visualized by means of integrated views. Thanks to the adoption of Model-Driven Engineering (MDE) techniques, these models drive the flexible execution of the final mobile app on target mobile devices. A prototype of the platform, making use of novel and advanced Web and mobile technologies, is also illustrated.

Keywords: Mobile mashups · Mashup modeling · Context modeling · Context-aware mobile applications · GraphQL

1 Introduction

The data deluge we are confronting today virtually drives people to continuously search and discover new information. The opportunity to access a large amount of information, however, does not always correspond to the growth of people knowledge. Many times, indeed, one does not know how to filter data "on-the-fly" to obtain the information that is the most suitable to the current context of use. This aspect is even more critical for mobile devices. Smart phones, for example, are often used to satisfy "quickly" very contingent information needs. Also their reduced screen size and battery power do not favor neither visualizing huge data sets nor executing multiple progressive queries to filter out irrelevant data.

Given this evidence, our research focuses on the definition of a methodology and related tools for the semi-automatic design and development of *Context-Aware Mobile mashUpS* (CAMUS) [1]. CAMUS leverage the results of two main

© Springer International Publishing AG 2017
F. Daniel and M. Gaedke (Eds.): RMC 2016, CCIS 696, pp. 108–128, 2017.
DOI: 10.1007/978-3-319-53174-8_7

research lines, related to the design of context-aware systems and mashups, with the aim to support developers in the creation of flexible apps that dynamically gather and combine data from heterogeneous data sources and filter and adapt the integrated content to the users' situational needs. With respect to traditional applications, designed to satisfy predefined requirements, the CAMUS added-value is their intrinsic capability of identifying pertinent data sources, i.e., adequate with respect to the current users' needs, and pervasively presenting them to the final user in the form of context-aware integrated visualizations deployed as mobile apps. This application paradigm overcomes the limits posed by pre-packaged apps and offers to the users flexible and personalized applications, whose structure and content may even emerge at runtime based on the actual user needs and situation of use.

In this paper we show how CAMUS design and development can be concretely based on a set of high-level abstractions for context and mashup modeling. In particular, we will present a novel design methodology and related tools for fast prototyping of mobile mashups, where context becomes a first-class design dimension supporting: *(i)* the identification of the most adequate resources that can satisfy the users' information needs and *(ii)* the consequent tailoring at runtime of the provided data and functions. We start from two consolidated approaches for context modeling [2,3] and mashup modeling [4] and show how the synergies of the two approaches can be amplified to define a new design methodology for the fast prototyping of flexible mobile apps.

This paper is organized as follows: Sect. 2 clarifies the motivations of our work and summarizes the main elements that characterize our design methodology by also comparing it with other similar approaches. Section 3 describes the main design steps based on the adoption of two consolidated approaches for context and mashup modeling, which are however integrated and somehow revisited or augmented to comply with each other's features. Section 4 illustrates the organization of the resulting framework, as well as the architecture and the implementation of the related platform supporting both the design of CAMUS apps, by means of visual design environments, and the context-aware execution of the generated mobile apps. Section 6 summarizes the main features of our design framework in relation to some classifying dimensions adopted during the Rapid Mashup Challenge. Section 7 then shortly describes the demo given during the challenge. Section 8 finally outlines our conclusions and describes our future work.

2   Rationale and Background

The CAMUS project merges techniques coming from two areas whose role is fundamental for the solution of problems related to the design of mobile systems. The first area deals with the issue of information overload by introducing *tailoring* techniques based on context-awareness, while the other one addresses the seamless integration of data and services. From different perspectives, both areas promote the creation of flexible mobile applications that dynamically gather and combine data from heterogeneous data sources, supporting the users' situational needs.

2.1   Context Awareness

The research on context made a significant step forward in the 90's, when the research community raised the problem of representing context-aware user and system activities [5]. While the community of computer science professionals initially perceived the context only as a matter of user location and time, this notion has been extended including, in the idea of context, other personalization aspects like current user interests, current role of the user in the system, the company the user keeps at the moment, and possibly other situational dimensions that may depend on the specific application at hand [6].

In CAMUS, the perspectives that characterize the different contextual situations in which the users can act in a given application scenario are modelled by means of the so-called *Context Dimension Model* [3], which provides the constructs to define at design-time the Universal Context Dimension Tree (*Universal CDT*). As represented in Fig. 1(a), the Universal CDT is a hierarchical structure consisting of *(i) context dimensions* (black nodes), modeling the different perspectives through which the user perceives the application domain (e.g., *time, interest topic, transport*), *(ii)* the allowed *dimension values* (white nodes), i.e., the values used to tailor the context-aware information (e.g., "morning", "with car", "culture"), and *(iii) variables* (e.g., "geographic coordinates" for a *location* dimension), that are either custom values supplied by the user at run-time or data acquired by device sensors (e.g., the current GPS coordinates of a given device). The dimension values and the variables are also called *context elements*. Note that the adoption of a hierarchical structure allows us to employ different abstraction levels to specify and represent contexts.

Any sub-tree of the Universal CDT with at most one element for each dimension represents *a possible user context*. Figure 1(b) shows a possible context for the Universal CDT of Fig. 1(a).

The CDT was originally introduced to tailor, at design time, the contextual portions of a global database, in order to grant to the users run-time, context-aware access to huge datasets. In this paper we will describe how, when a certain context is detected at run-time by means of device sensors or using some information provided by the user, the context-relevant services are invoked to build a service mashup appropriate for the identified context.

2.2   Mobile Mashups

Mashups are "composite" applications constructed by integrating ready-to-use functions and content exposed by public or private services and Web APIs [7]. The mashup composition paradigm was initially exploited in the consumer Web for creating rapidly simple Web applications that reused programmable APIs and content scraped out from other Web pages. Soon the potential of this lightweight integration practice emerged in the other domains where the possibility

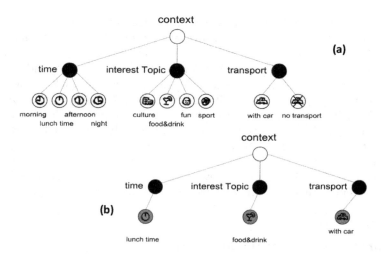

Fig. 1. Example of Universal CDT and a possible context.

to create rapidly new applications, also by laypeople, is an important requirement. In the last years many efforts have been devoted to the definition of usable and intuitive composition paradigms. This aspect is indeed considered a factor enabling the addition of significant new value with respect to other development practices. Intuitive notations and visual design environments can offer the advantage for designers, or even end users, to achieve effective applications that match exactly their needs and that can be created in a short time by simply reusing and customizing existing resources. Therefore, several approaches have proposed composition paradigms based on visual notations that abstract relevant mashup development aspects and reduce- or sometimes totally eliminate, the need of programming.

Among the proposed approaches for mashup design, very few specifically concentrate on mobile mashups. In [8] the authors illustrate a mobile generator system that aims to support fast prototyping as it is able to automatically generate a large part of the application code. However, this approach does not support content integration, while we believe this is a fundamental feature for the mobile usage context where integrated views can greatly improve the information access experience. Also, it proposes a domain specific language with abstractions that are very close to the ones of the Android execution platform. The approach indeed focuses exclusively on Android apps and does not exploit modeling as a means to abstract from specific technology and achieve multi-platform deployment.

Recently proposed services, like IFTTT (If This Than That - https://ifttt. com/wtf) and Atooma (http://www.atooma.com), enable users to synchronize the behavior of different apps through simple conditional statements. However, they do not support at all the integration of different data sets and of the corresponding UIs.

For the design of CAMUS apps, we adopt the approach presented in [4]. It is based on a UI-centric paradigm for data integration, as it requires acting directly on the user interface of the mashup under construction, in a kind of live-programming paradigm where each composition action corresponds to a data integration operation that generates an immediate visual feedback on the artifact under construction [9,10]. One of its distinguishing features is the capability of abstracting from the specific technologies of the target applications. In line with the Model-Driven Engineering (MDE) philosophy, it indeed leverages on the generation of application schemas, and on their interpretation in different execution platforms by means of engines supporting the generation of code for native application. This is a very relevant feature: recent studies on device and traffic share report on a generally observed attitude of users to access applications through different devices (desktop and mobile) [11].

2.3   Context-Aware Mobile Mashups

The literature reports different experiences for the development of context-aware mobile applications, showing how applications can be extended to gather and use context at run-time (see for example [12]). However, these works consider context-awareness as an orthogonal dimension, to be programmed *ad-hoc* for any application, while they do not provide conceptual models and design frameworks.

In [13] the authors show how a mashup design environment may implicitly provide support for context-awareness, thanks to the introduction of mashup components in charge of managing context, i.e., capturing context events and activating related operations in other components of the mashup. Although effective, the approach does not provide any abstraction to model the context; the designer is in charge of configuring the context components (basically location and time) by means of parameter settings. We instead assign a fundamental role to usage-situation modeling, from which we then derive the logics for selecting services and dynamically build the final applications.

MyService is a mashup design framework that supports the creation of context-aware services based on rules [14]. It provides an Android design environment that allows end users to select pre-defined context-based recommendation rules on top of a service directory. Proper services are thus selected depending on the context gathered at runtime, and the code of a mashup is generated. This approach is in line with our idea to filter at runtime services by means of a context representation. However, MyService focuses especially on location-based adaptations, while we are able to cover any dimension that can filter content. The CDT model indeed is generic with respect to the specific domain, allowing for the representation of all possible perspectives that characterize context by means of the generic concept of *context dimension*. Also, MyService does not support data integration and it is not clear whether the generated code also covers the rendering of User Interface views. In the following sections we will show how we address this point – which is crucial especially when different execution platforms are addressed – by means of advanced technologies that instantiate views in the mobile app starting form an abstract schema of the integrated data set to be provided by the app.

3 The CAMUS Methodology

We now present the design methodology for the creation of CAMUS apps starting from the specification of context requirements. Our approach is characterized by the adoption of design environments that, in line with recent approaches to visual programming of mashups, make intensive use of high-level visual abstractions [4,15]. Visual paradigms indeed hide the complexity typical of service composition, data integration and the programming of context-aware mobile apps, and assist CAMUS designers (even if non-experts in these technologies) in the creation of multi-device personalized applications.

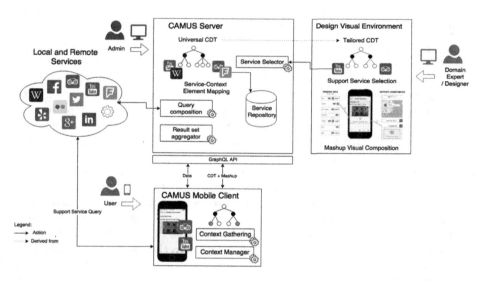

Fig. 2. Main system components and supported design and execution activities in CAMUS.

Figure 2 represents the general organization of the design framework and highlights the flow of the different activities and related artifacts that enable the transition from high-level modeling notations to running code. In the sequel, we will describe the activities performed by three main personae, the *administrator*, the *mashup designer* and the *app user*, who are the main actors interacting with the framework at different levels and with different goals. In order to exemplify how these activities are carried out, we will refer to a case study in the domain of tourism, characterized by: *(i)* a tourism *service provider*, who sets up an ecosystem of tourism services and the platform for the delivery of CAMUS apps; *(ii)* the *tourist*, i.e., the end user of a CAMUS app created on top of the available services; and *(iii)* a *tour agent*, i.e., an intermediary player who assists the end user in the creation of the specific tour and, consequently, acts as mash-up designer customizing the CAMUS app according to preferences related to the specific trip and person - which might not be entirely captured by the Universal CDT.

3.1 Creation of the Service Ecosystem

The *administrator* is in charge of managing the CAMUS server and resources. One of the main roles is to create and maintain the *service repository*. S/He registers into the platform distributed resources (remote APIs or in-house services) that are pertinent with respect to a given domain, as resulting from the specific requirements and from the requests of the final users. For example, in the tourism domain the administrator will register services that provide information about hotel, restaurants, points of interest, and any other information useful for a trip. Service registration is taken by creating descriptors that specify:

- *How the resources are to be invoked*, e.g., the service endpoint, its operations and input parameters. In this phase, some parameters can be bound to wrappers that perform transformations from symbolic context values gathered at runtime to corresponding numerical service input. Figure 3 reports an excerpt of a descriptor for a service returning data on events. The input parameter `price` is associated with a wrapper that transforms symbolic terms, such as `low`, `medium` and `high` specified as user preferences, into specific price values, as expected by the service.
- *The schema of the responses of the returned service.* To ensure homogeneity of data formats, needed to merge the data that must be visualized by the final app, the response schema of each registered service is annotated with *terms* (e.g., *title*, *description*, *address*) indicating categories of attributes, according to a vocabulary that is defined and maintained in the service repository. These annotating terms have a double role: when the mashup is defined (see Sect. 3.3), they allow the designer to select service attributes by reasoning on abstract categories, instead of specific attributes resulting from service queries; at run time they assist the merging progress of different result sets, since it is easier to identify attributes that refer to the same entity properties.

For these annotations we currently assume the availability of a set of *ad-hoc* defined category tags, which the administrator explicitly associates to the attributes returned by registered services. Domain ontologies can of course be exploited as well to automatically associate service attributes to semantic terms.

3.2 Universal CDT Augmentation

The *administrator* also specifies the Universal CDT, providing a representation of all the possible usage contexts. In order to support the context-aware selection of services at runtime, s/he augments the Universal CDT by defining *mappings*

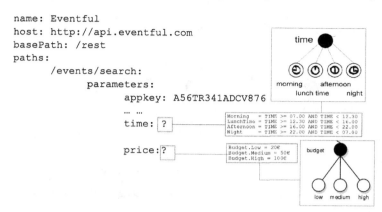

```
name: Eventful
host: http://api.eventful.com
basePath: /rest
paths:
    /events/search:
        parameters:
            appkey: A56TR341ADCV876
        ... ...
        time: [?]
        price:[?]
```

Fig. 3. An excerpt of a service descriptor specifying properties for service invocation.

between the identified context elements and the services registered in the platform.

Services belong to two different categories. *Core services* provide the main data that contribute to forming the core content of the final app. As represented in Fig. 4, they are associated with the so-called *primary dimensions*, i.e., dimensions for whose values some "primary' content" has to be provided in the final application. Such content is considered as primary as it is supposed to be the main object of the users' requests. For example, services providing data on restaurants are associated with the food&drink value of the interest topic dimension. Therefore, their selection at runtime occurs if the food&drink dimension is the emerging user interest in the identified context.

Support services supply auxiliary content (e.g., the meteo condition or the public transportation in a given location) or functionality (e.g., the localization on a map of a restaurant retrieved by some core service).

Do consider that, when the app is working, the available support services may vary depending on the usage context. This means that, during the Universal CDT augmentation, the association is operated *at the service category level*. For example, a "transport" service category is associated with a given context node (e.g., food&drink) to represent that, within the final mashups, transport services will be selected when the user's context is characterized by the food&drink interest topic. Then, at runtime a specific service belonging to this category will be selected and invoked, based on the identified geographical area. This requires specifying, within the service descriptor, the category the service belongs to and its characterization with respect to the context values its final selection depends on. So, during The Universal CDT augmentation, the administrator characterizes the role that every node in the Universal CDT plays in the runtime selection of services, by assigning two typologies: *filter* or *ranking*. By default, all the nodes have a *filter* role, meaning that reaching them while traversing the tree implies adding a corresponding filter for service selection. The administrator

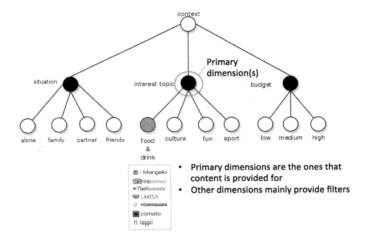

Fig. 4. An excerpt of a service descriptor specifying properties for service invocation.

can characterize some nodes as *ranking* when they can provide a ranking criteria for sorting different candidate services. For example, *location* is a ranking node because its related context parameters might influence the selection of services that provide relevant data in a given geographical area (e.g., the information services provided by the local transportation company of a certain city are to be preferred to a generic transport information service).

3.3 Mashup Visual Design

The *mashUp designer* starts from the image of the available resources represented by the augmented Universal CDT and, using a *Design Visual Environment*, defines a *Tailored CDT* by further refining the selection of possible contexts and the mapping with services (both core and support). This is needed to fulfill the needs and preferences of specific users or user groups.

Given the services associated with a given context dimension (e.g., all the services providing data on restaurants associated with the food&drink context dimension) the designer can select the categories of attributes (i.e., the annotating terms specified at service-registration time) to be visualized in the mobile app. As schematically represented in Fig. 5, this selection is operated visually, according to a composition paradigm for mobile mashup creation already defined and implemented in the PEUDOM mashup tool [4]. The designer drags and drops the semantic terms associated with the attributes of the service response. A "virtual device" provides an immediate representation of how the final app will be shown on the client device. In addition, the designer can include *support services* that can provide additional information and enrich the user experience (e.g., provide transport indications to reach a restaurant, or extend the core content with descriptions of places taken from Wikipedia). Support services are also context dependent: for instance, if the user expresses that s/he is in a situation where s/he wants to use "transportation by car", the system provides route information; otherwise, if s/he selects "public transport" it suggests a bus line. This requires that also for support services the inclusion of data attributes be operated by exploiting annotating terms describing attribute categories exposed by classes of services, not the actual data attributes exposed by single, specific services. At runtime, the binding defined at service registration time between semantic terms and service attributes will be exploited to query the services actually selected.

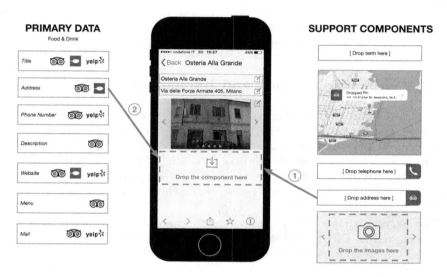

Fig. 5. Schematic representation of the visual mapping activities to associate service attribute classes to elements of the final app UI.

All the visual design actions are translated by the design environment in a JSON-based *mashup schema*, which specifies rules that at runtime guide the instantiation of the resulting app and the creation of its views.

It is worth noting that, in comparison to other approaches to mashup design [7], the composition activity and, more specifically, the selection of services are not exclusively driven by the functional characteristics of the available services or by the compatibility of their input and output parameters. Rather, the initial specification of context requirements enables first the progressive filtering of services and then the tailoring of service data to support the final situations of use.

3.4 App Execution

The *CAMUS (app) users* are the final recipients of the mobile app that offers a different bouquet of content and functions in each different situation of use.

When the app is executed, the context elements that characterize the current situation, identified by means of a client-side *sensor wrapper* or explicitly selected by the user, are communicated to the server; this, in turn, chooses the pertinent services to be invoked and returns an integrated data set that includes the attributes corresponding to the semantic terms selected during the mashup design. The mashup schema created by the designer is thus interpreted locally on the device (by means of a *Schema Interpreter*), and the generated views are populated with the returned data as defined during the visual mapping step. The platform indeed exploits generative techniques: modeling abstractions guide the design of the final applications, while generative layers mediate between high-level visual models and low-level engines that execute the final mashups. Execution engines, created as hybrid-native applications for different mobile devices, then make it possible the interpretation and pervasive execution of schemas.

4   Platform Organization and Implementation

In order to support the CAMUS methodology, we developed a proof-of-concept prototype; the demo given at the Rapid Mashup Challenge focused on it. Its architecture is server-centric, meaning that a *Server* manages the main functions for the execution of the mobile app, i.e.: *(i)* analyzing of the user's context, detected through the mobile device, to select the services to be queried and, *(ii)* querying the selected services and transforming their results into an integrated data set to be rendered by the mobile app.

The Server exposes several endpoints to enable the execution of service queries as well as CRUD operations on other system data, such as users' profiles, and the descriptors for the Universal CDT and the service repository. The framework used for its implementation is Node.js and the database is MongoDB. The main API invoked by the mobile client to access the server functionality is compliant with the GraphQL API specification [16]. GraphQL offers a layer that enforces a set of custom-defined typing rules on the data sent and received via HTTP. Besides, it provides a flexible way to specify the response format, by making it easier to support different generations of APIs.

The *Visual Design Environment* consists of a suite of Web applications to: *(i)* easily register new services to the system, *(ii)* specify visually (and automatically generate an internal representation of) the CDTs and the associations of services with pertinent nodes, and *(iii)* design visually the final mashups and automatically generate their schema.

The *Client App* is the front-end enabling the interaction of the end-user with the whole system. During its initialization, the app loads the user CDT and the JSON-based specification of mashup schemas to be rendered from the server. The schema specifies the structure of the app views and drives their instantiation. The transformation of the schema into concrete views exploits React Native [17], a framework recently introduced by Facebook to streamline the production of cross-platform mobile apps. The app logic is written in Javascript and, for the most part, is agnostic with respect to the target platform. React enforces a pseudo-functional/reactive approach that involves a central state (which holds the *model* of the application) and a number of pure functions that render the view. The view elements, in turn, can produce actions that act on the state through a dispatcher, while network responses represent another source of actions that can change the state. The state of the app serves the rendering of the views and their data: it is mainly composed of the mashup data, the current interest topic, the CDT and the result of the current context-based query.

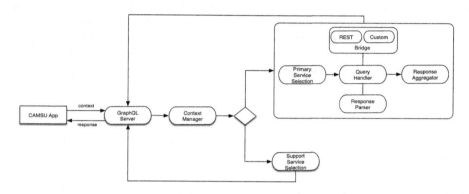

Fig. 6. Server request flow.

A typical *request* from the client is composed of a JSON payload that describes the *context* and a specification of the format of the data that is expected by the client. As represented in Fig. 6, the request is thus processed through the following steps:

- The *Context Manager* parses the context and "decorates" it with all the Augmented UCDT information (services, ranks, etc.) related to its elements.
- Based on the analyzed context, the *Primary Service Selection* component selects the services to be queried.
- The *Query Handler* queries the selected services by using service-specific bridges that wrap the retrieved result sets and transform them into a common internal representation that complies with the semantic terms associated to the different service attributes. This internal representation enables merging the different data sets based on attributes associated with the same terms.
- Finally, the activation of support services – if any –, is bound to the selection of specific attributes in the integrated result set, as defined by the mashup designer when creating the mashup.

The rest of this section will illustrate in more details the steps involved in the request flow.

Primary Service Selection. As mentioned above, the *Context Manager* takes care of decorating the user's current context with the information coming from the Augmented Universal CDT. Service selection is thus operated by interpreting the request context as a key-value query, and using this representation to "navigate" through the Universal CDT specification. The result of this navigation is the set of *Service Associations* (*SA*) found in the different visited nodes, that suggest the use of service that can be pertinent with respect to the current context. Each association is composed by the priority that characterizes the service for the reached node and the node weight. These values are set when the Universal CDT is modeled: the priority is an increasing integer starting from 1, and weights are predefined values assigned with the constraint that a filter node's weight must be less than that of a ranking node. The final relevance value for each service s is thus computed from the weights w_i and node priorities p_i as:

$$R_s = \sum_{i \in SA(s)} \frac{w_i}{p_i} \tag{1}$$

The obtained value is used to rank and filter the N top relevant services for the query.

Query Handling. The *Query Handler* is in charge of identifying the queries to be posed to the selected services; a number of bridges than actually invoke the services by formulating the queries in accordance with the protocol exposed by the service APIs. We supply a default bridge for REST-type services plus an abstract class that can be extended for implementing new bridges covering further service types.

A bridge receives the service descriptor provided by the Query Handler and builds the URL where the service should be queried. During this composition, the bridge uses the context to retrieve the list of parameter nodes which, in turn, store the values that are needed to perform the query. When all the necessary queries are completed, it sends the responses obtained back to the Query Handler.

Response Aggregation. The *Response Aggregator* executes two main tasks: *(i)* merging items from different services that refer to a same instance and *(ii)* scoring each instance. In fact, two or more services might return data referring to a same instance, thus duplicate identification is needed to discover equal or similar instances and fuse them into a unique object. The fusion then might produce a richer set of attributes for an instance, as one service can provide attributes not supplied by the others.

Merging is computationally intensive, since it requires pairwise comparison of all the instances in any of the service result set. To reduce this complexity we devised some optimizations: first, each instance item is classified on the basis of the phonetic code of its key attribute (for example, the title), using some phonetic string matching metrics[1]. Then, inside each class, pairwise comparison of the common attributes is used to compute a similarity index. If this value is greater than a predefined threshold, the two items are considered similar and they are fused together. The complexity of this comparison strategy is $O(n)$ (i.e., linear in the number of analyzed instances).

Support Service Selection. The selection of support services is similar to the one operated for primary services. However, a support service is selected and included in the mashup if and only if all the bindings defined between the mashup core data and the operations exposed by the support service, as defined by the mashup designer, are satisfied. This avoids runtime invocation of services that are not applicable in a particular context, for instance because the needed input parameters are not provided by the integrated result set or by the usage context. The result of the support service selection is a set of service endpoints that are communicated to the client within the mashup schema, so that the mobile app can directly invoke the services to retrieve and visualize the auxiliary data.

App Life Cycle. At the application startup, the user chooses the current interest topic. The context selection page supports the user in editing the current context, and also probes the hardware for sensors data. When the user finalizes the context input, a GraphQL query is built and sent to the server. The request specifies the structure the incoming data should have in order to be rendered in the results page. An important difference with respect to a more traditional approach like REST is that different clients can request different data formats from the same end point. Once received, the data is stored in the main application state and the app view is re-rendered by hydrating a React Native template.

The view schema provides a very flexible mashup design. As reported in Fig. 7, every page is associated with the corresponding key in the file (e.g.: `results`, `details`, ...) and, at render time, the view builder loads the schema dedicated to the rendering of data for the current topic (tag `topics`); potentially, the app is able to render a different view for each possible topic. The tag `contents` specifies the view elements; thanks to the `style` attribute it is possible to pass directly to the app CSS-like style attributes used in React. The elements within the `contents` tag are defined recursively, thus enabling a very customizable design of the app: in principle, any single view element can be defined in this way and then dynamically instantiated.

5   Evaluation

In this section we provide a preliminary characterization of the performance of the system. Since the application is still under active development, the numbers shown here are to be considered with care. However, we think that they provide

---

[1] Our current prototype uses the Chapman's Soundex metrics [18].

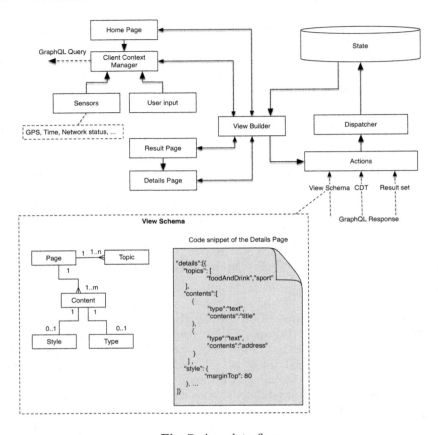

Fig. 7. App data flow.

some interesting insights on the feasibility of context-aware strategies for service selection and querying, as the ones illustrated in the previous sections.

System and Workload Model. To model the system, we use a basic $M/G/1$ queue [19]. In fact our system behaves as:

- $M/*/*$: a service node where request arrival follows a *markovian* process, i.e. requests arrive continuously and independently at a constant average rate λ. We will use this assumption in the characterization of the response time.
- $*/G/*$: the service rate distribution is not yet known, so we assume it being a general distribution with fixed mean and variance.
- $*/*/1$: a single process (Node.js) serves incoming requests.

The system used for workload evaluation is characterized by an Intel Core i5-5257U CPU, with 2 cores and a 3 GHz frequency, a 8 GB DDR3 RAM, and an SSD disk of 128 GB.

Service Time. The service time is the time it takes for a single request to be served. To better understand the distribution of the service time (which has been assumed as *general* in the previous paragraph), we use a sequence of 500 back-to-back requests, where each request is sent once the previous one has been served. Requests are served by the system with a first-come/first served (FCFS) policy. We stubbed the *query handler* in such a way as to measure just the internal delays of the system components.

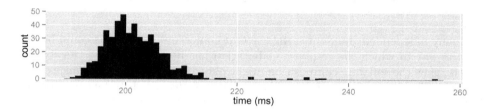

Fig. 8. Distribution of the service time.

Figure 8 shows the histogram of the measured response time. To a first inspection, the shape of the distribution seems to agree with a log-normal distribution whose parameters are $\mu = 202(\text{ms}), \sigma = 6.4(\text{ms})$. This suggests an ability to sustain almost 5 requests per second. We use this information to generate a workload of independent requests.

Response Time. When receiving independent requests (which can arrive before the current one is effectively served), the system can show a delay due to requests queuing up. To characterize the behavior under this type of workload, we generate a sequence of requests using an exponential arrival-rate distribution. The exponential distribution is in fact congruent with the markovian arrival-rate assumption made above:

$$f(x; \lambda) = \lambda e^{-\lambda x}, \text{where } x \geq 0$$

where λ characterizes the rate of generation of independent requests and x is the time between one request and the next.

Figure 9 shows the box-plot charts for a varying request rate, from 1 to 5 requests per seconds (saturation threshold). As can be seen, the system exhibits a robust response up to $\lambda < 4$. After that point, both variance and mean of the response time exponentially diverge, approaching the saturation point individuated in the previous paragraph.

Discussion. The above analysis brings us to an interesting insight which we are going to investigate further in our work: the service time is log-normally distributed. This type of distribution is characteristic of a process which is a product

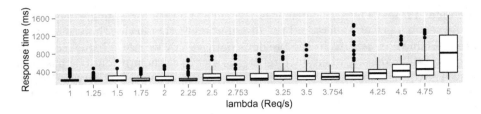

Fig. 9. Distribution of the response time under varying workload.

of many independent random variables. Our conjecture is that this could be due to the way in which the response elaboration has been split across the components, thus the software composition might play a role in the performance of the system. This is however a preliminary observation that needs to be corroborated by means of wider and deeper investigation.

6   Features and Level of Maturity

We now summarize the main characteristics of our design approach in relation to some dimensions for the classification of mashup paradigms used at the Rapid Mashup Challenge. Our approach mainly supports the generation of *data mashups*. The platform backend indeed exploits data fusion techniques to combine the data sets extracted from the selected core services. This process involves mainly the invocation of *data components*. However, the generated mashups also include mechanisms for *UI synchronization*: an event-driven logic at the UI level is used to activate the generation and synchronization of different views in the app. For example, when an item is selected in a view displaying core data, a new view is instantiated to display related support data.

The execution of the generated mashup is *distributed between the mobile app and the backend server*. Besides capturing the context parameters and composing the requests to the backend, the app is also in charge of interpreting the mashup schema and instantiating corresponding views. The identification of pertinent services and the generation of the mashup schema is however executed by the server. The integration logics is based on an *orchestration of the involved services*: decoupled components are indeed invoked by the Query Handler, according to a schema determined by the selection of the primary and support services. The resulting mashups are *short-living* as the involved services and the way they are integrated in the app depend on the current context, which is reconsidered at any new requests generated by the app. However, the app allows the user to materialize on the server some data, like reservation data and tickets, that can be useful for future sessions.

The tool assisting the design of CAMUS apps targets *both developers and non-programmers*: the former (e.g., the platform administrators having experience with service registration and requirements modeling) are supposed to prepare the instruments (e.g., the CDT specification) that the latter can visually refine according to a *WYISIWIG visual language,* to better capture the requirements of the specific usage domain. The design tool then offers a *full automation* for the generation of the final app starting from the schemas visually defined by the mashup designers.

Any change to the schemas requires a *re-initialization of the final app.* Our composition approach, indeed, supports live programming during the app design, as it offers a preview of the final app in a virtual device where each composition action is "materialized" into a change visible in the app UI. However, once an application schema is downloaded on a mobile device, the local execution engine keeps instantiating the app according to that schema. Possible changes will be applied only if a new execution of the app starts (and a new schema is downloaded on the device).

While we have a stable implementation of the platform backend and of the app runtime, we still need efforts to achieve an integrated visual design environment. At the time of the demo at the Rapid Mashup Challenge, all the JSON descriptors (service descriptors and CDT representation) had to be written manually. We have now started developing visual editors for service registration and for the CDT specification. The PEUDOM visual editor [4] assists the visual mapping activity for the design of the app views; however, we still need to reconcile the syntactic format of the mashup schema generated by the design tool with the one required by the current app execution engine.

7   Demo at the Rapid Mashup Challenge

As explained above, we still do not have an integrated visual design environment, since our research so far has especially focused on proving the feasibility of the approach for the context-driven, dynamic selection of services. Therefore, at the Rapid Mashup Challenge we illustrated the main features of the design methodology: we emphasized the role that context modeling plays in the dynamic selection of services and showed that the context-driven, dynamic construction of mobile mashups is feasible. The dynamic generation of CAMUS apps starting from the representation of possible usage situations is indeed the most characterizing feature of our approach.

During the presentation we illustrated the steps needed to set up the service ecosystem, as well as the mechanisms that, starting from the context captured at run-time and the representation of the augmented CDT, enable *(i)* the selection of pertinent services, *(ii)* the production of a result set integrating data extracted from the single services, and *(iii)* the dynamic generation of the mobile app views for data visualization.

Figure 10 shows the sequence of app views that were shown during the challenge to illustrate such mechanisms. The first view (Fig. 10(a)) allows the user to select an interest topic; this selection plus other parameters characterizing the usage situations (e.g., time and geographical position) are sent to the platform back-end and trigger the selection of pertinent services. In case of multiple selected services, data fusion procedures are also executed; thus the composed

(a) View for the Interest Topic selection   (b) View displaying search results   (c) View for data and functions offered by support services

Fig. 10. App screenshots from the demonstration.

result set is sent back to the client, where it is displayed through the view illustrated in Fig. 10(b). Finally, the view in Fig. 10(c) shows further details made available by support services (in the example GoogleMaps and the device-local dialing service) for an item selected in the previous view.

The steps undertaken by the server that correspond to the previous interaction flow, and especially the actions to manage the context and to instantiate the app views, can be seen in the video available at: https://www.dropbox.com/s/nitnsehsv38x5co/demo%20camus.mov?dl=0.

8 Conclusions

This paper illustrates the CAMUS methodology and its related platform, whose aim is to empower non-expert developers to create context-aware, mobile apps by integrating multiple and heterogeneous APIs acting on situational needs. It discusses in particular the major role that the CAMUS design approach gives to context modeling. The specification of the Universal CDT is the central design activity; around it the construction of the mashup is performed. At design time the designer defines mashup schemas by reasoning at a high level of abstraction on possible context dimensions and associated service categories; at execution time, specific services are dynamically selected and integrated by taking into account the actual user context. The paper also discusses how taking into account context elements in the automatic instantiation of the final app, and especially selecting on the fly the services to be queried, is feasible and does not affect the performance of the server components.

This paper does not discuss the usability of the design methodology (i.e., how the methodology is perceived by designers) and the usability of the generated apps (i.e., if they are considered useful and usable by the end users). However, since the CAMUS framework still exploits the composition paradigms and the final app organization that we already defined in our previous work, we capitalize on the large body of data and user feedback collected in the last years through families of user studies (see for example [4,15] for an extensive discussion on the conducted evaluations). Our current work is devoted to refining the implementation of the platform, and especially to defining a tight integration among the different visual design environments that we developed so far. Other efforts are being devoted to the formal characterization of the operations for service selection and composition based on the CDT representation.

Acknowledgments. This research is partially supported by the research grants FluidCAMUS, funded by Aliday S.p.A., and SHELL (CTN01 00128 111357), funded by the Italian Ministry for University and Research - MIUR. We like to thank the large group of students of Politecnico di Milano who enthusiastically contributed to the design and implementation of the first CAMUS prototype. They allowed us to assess the feasibility of revising mashup composition practices through the introduction of context modeling concepts.

References

1. Corvetta, F., Matera, M., Medana, R., Quintarelli, E., Rizzo, V., Tanca, L.: Designing and developing context-aware mobile mashups: the CAMUS approach. In: Cimiano, P., Frasincar, F., Houben, G.-J., Schwabe, D. (eds.) ICWE 2015. LNCS, vol. 9114, pp. 651–654. Springer, Heidelberg (2015). doi:10.1007/978-3-319-19890-3_49
2. Bolchini, C., Orsi, G., Quintarelli, E., Schreiber, F.A., Tanca, L.: Context modeling and context awareness: steps forward in the context-addict project. IEEE Data Eng. Bull. **34**(2), 47–54 (2011)
3. Bolchini, C., Curino, C., Orsi, G., Quintarelli, E., Rossato, R., Schreiber, F.A., Tanca, L.: And what can context do for data? Commun. ACM **52**(11), 136–140 (2009)
4. Cappiello, C., Matera, M., Picozzi, M.: A ui-centric approach for the end-user development of multidevice mashups. TWEB **9**(3), 11 (2015)
5. Abowd, G.D., Dey, A.K., Brown, P.J., Davies, N., Smith, M., Steggles, P.: Towards a better understanding of context and context-awareness. In: Gellersen, H.-W. (ed.) HUC 1999. LNCS, vol. 1707, pp. 304–307. Springer, Heidelberg (1999). doi:10.1007/3-540-48157-5_29
6. Bolchini, C., Curino, C., Quintarelli, E., Schreiber, F.A., Tanca, L.: A data-oriented survey of context models. SIGMOD Rec. **36**(4), 19–26 (2007)
7. Daniel, F., Matera, M.: Mashups - Concepts, Models and Architectures. Data-Centric Systems and Applications. Springer, Heidelberg (2014)

8. Chaisatien, P., Prutsachainimmit, K., Tokuda, T.: Mobile mashup generator system for cooperative applications of different mobile devices. In: Auer, S., Díaz, O., Papadopoulos, G.A. (eds.) ICWE 2011. LNCS, vol. 6757, pp. 182–197. Springer, Heidelberg (2011). doi:10.1007/978-3-642-22233-7_13

9. Cappiello, C., Matera, M., Picozzi, M., Caio, A., Guevara, M.T.: Mobimash: end user development for mobile mashups. In: Proceedings of the 21st World Wide Web Conference, WWW 2012, Lyon, France, 16–20 April 2012 (Companion Volume), pp. 473–474. ACM (2012)

10. Cappiello, C., Matera, M., Picozzi, M.: End-user development of mobile mashups. In: Marcus, A. (ed.) DUXU 2013. LNCS, vol. 8015, pp. 641–650. Springer, Heidelberg (2013). doi:10.1007/978-3-642-39253-5_71

11. Lella, A., Lipsman, A., Martin, B.: The 2015 U.S. Mobile App Report. White Paper, ComScore. http://www.comscore.com/Insights/Presentations-and-Whitepapers/2015/The-2015-US-Mobile-App-Report

12. Schaller, R.: Mobile tourist guides: bridging the gap between automation and users retaining control of their itineraries. In: Proceedings of the 5th Information Interaction in Context Symposium, IIiX 2014, pp. 320–323. ACM, New York (2014)

13. Daniel, F., Matera, M.: Mashing up context-aware web applications: a component-based development approach. In: Bailey, J., Maier, D., Schewe, K.-D., Thalheim, B., Wang, X.S. (eds.) WISE 2008. LNCS, vol. 5175, pp. 250–263. Springer, Heidelberg (2008). doi:10.1007/978-3-540-85481-4_20

14. Lee, E., Joo, H.J.: Developing lightweight context-aware service mashup applications. In: 2013 15th International Conference on Advanced Communication Technology (ICACT), pp. 1060–1064, January 2013

15. Ardito, C., Costabile, M.F., Desolda, G., Lanzilotti, R., Matera, M., Piccinno, A., Picozzi, M.: User-driven visual composition of service-based interactive spaces. J. Vis. Lang. Comput. **25**(4), 278–296 (2014)

16. Facebook: GraphQL. Draft RFC Specification, Facebook (2015). https://facebook.github.io/graphql

17. Facebook: React Native. React Native official page, Facebook (2015). https://facebook.github.io/react-native

18. Zobel, J., Dart, P.: Phonetic string matching: lessons from information retrieval. In: Proceedings of the 19th Annual International ACM SIGIR Conference on Research and Development in Information Retrieval, SIGIR 1996, 166–172. ACM, New York (1996)

19. Sundarapandian, V.: Probability, Statistics and Queuing Theory. PHI Learning, New Delhi (2009)

Challenge Outcome and Conclusion

Martin Gaedke[1] and Florian Daniel[2(✉)]

[1] Technische Universität Chemnitz, Str. der Nationen 62, 09111 Chemnitz, Germany
`martin.gaedke@informatik.tu-chemnitz.de`
[2] Politecnico di Milano, Via Ponzio 34/5, 20133 Milano, Italy
`florian.daniel@polimi.it`

Abstract. In this final chapter, we report on the outcome of the ICWE 2016 Rapid Mashup Challenge (RMC), describe the voting system used, and draw some conclusions regarding the presented works.

Keywords: Mashups · Challenge · Benchmarking

1 Challenge Organization

We recall that every tool participating in the challenge was allocated 20 min that the authors could split freely into a presentation of the demonstrated approach and the demonstration itself. The goal of the presentation was to introduce the approach and/or tool, to illustrate its design and to enumerate its most important features, so that the audience would be prepared for the actual demonstration. The live demonstration, in fact, aimed at showcasing the on-the-fly development of a mashup chosen by the authors in front of the audience. The starting point for all demonstrations was an empty workspace or a code editor in which the components/resources to be reused in the mashup had been pre-registered and pre-defined, but not yet assembled. Some authors chose to follow an iterative process, whereby the mashup was grown incrementally, piece by piece. Others also included a more general overview of the mashup tool capabilities, which was useful to demonstrate the expressive power of the tool, but did not necessarily help them build the most impressive mashup during the allocated time frame.

Each time a mashup was completed and the time for the demonstration had expired, the audience had the opportunity to ask questions to the authors. This interactive session was very useful to provide the mashup authors with valuable feedback and the audience with clarifications regarding what it had just seen during the demonstration. At the end of the interactive session, the audience could provide its assessment of the approach via simple ratings collected through the ASQ system. The results were aggregated on the fly and the overall ranking updated and shown to the audience and the tool authors.

F. Daniel and M. Gaedke (Eds.): RMC 2016, CCIS 696, pp. 129–134, 2017.
DOI: 10.1007/978-3-319-53174-8_8

2   The ASQ Voting System

The challenge evaluation phase was supported by the ASQ system [1]. ASQ (a permutation over Slides-Questions-Answers) allows anyone with a Web browser to follow a slideshow presentation and interact with the content by answering questions embedded in the slides. It was originally developed at the USI Faculty of Informatics to support in-classroom teaching activities by taking advantage of the fact that every student comes with his/her laptop to follow the lectures. Students not only can better read the content broadcast to their devices, but teachers can get real-time feedback about their level of understanding and thus adapt their pace and explanation depth during the lecture.

As such ASQ is a general tool and can be used also for any interactive presentation. In particular for the 2016 edition of the RMC, we reused the ASQ system already extended for the prior edition of the challenge. The extensions required were: (i) a special question type to gather ratings, over a 5-star scale, with the possibility to award also half stars; and (ii) a count-down timer activated at the beginning of each presentation/demo session to ensure every participant demonstrates his/her tool during the same amount of time.

The use of ASQ during the RMC enabled the easy involvement of the whole audience in the assessment of the presented approaches (including the authors themselves, who did however not vote in their own turn). A secondary benefit was that ASQ allows one to automate and increase the efficiency of the scoring process, where the answers are aggregated and the final ranking is recomputed after every participant is evaluated. The slides showing the metadata about the current participants (name of approach/tool, authors, abstract) were interleaved with the questions to evaluate them. This helped focusing the audience's attention and build a shared awareness of the proceedings of the challenge and to manage the time without introducing unnecessary delays.

3   Evaluation Criteria

In line with the call for participation of the RMC, every demonstration was evaluated according to five different criteria:

1. *Expressive power.* Each approach presented during the Challenge was accompanied by a filled feature checklist (introduced in the first chapter of this volume), which provided insight into the respective expressive power as declared by the authors. This year, we used the feature checklists only to select candidates before the Challenge, while during the Challenge we asked the audience to provide a subjective impression of the expressive power perceived. The more composition features an approach supports, the higher its expressive power.
2. *Flexibility.* This criterion aimed to assess the extensibility and adaptability of the approaches to different, possibly novel requirements. Although by now it is almost a decade that researchers have been working on mashups, every day

new requirements and/or technologies pop up, and mashup tools are perhaps the instruments that are exposed most to this evolution. Flexibility is thus paramount. The lower the effort needed to extend/adapt an approach to novel requirements, the higher the flexibility.

3. *Maturity.* On the other hand, given a development instrument, it is important to understand its level of maturity, that is, the stability and readiness for production of the instrument. This is perhaps the criterion that varied most among the presented approaches in the 2016 edition of the RMC, and it was important to capture the difference of maturity among the approaches in order to enable the reader to properly interpret the presented results. The closer an instrument is to a production-ready system, the higher its maturity.

4. *Intuitiveness.* This criterion explored the end-user perspective of mashup development with the presented approaches and tried to quantify how the audience perceived the respective ease of use in practical settings. Of course, the more graphical and interactive an approach, the fewer skills are needed to operate it, and the higher its intuitiveness.

5. *Demo effectiveness.* The last criterion aimed to assess the effectiveness of the showcased mashup scenario and demonstration in convincing the audience of the power of the presented approach/tool. Partly, this criterion therefore also includes the "performance" of the presenter. So, the more the audience understood the demonstration, the higher the demo effectiveness.

These criteria are different from those used in the 2015 edition of the Challenge, as the overall setting of the comparison was different (less restricted demonstrations and, hence, harder to compare) and the presented approaches were more heterogeneous among each other (again, harder to compare).

4   Results

Going straight to the point, Table 1 summarizes the feedback obtained from the audience by each of the tools participating in the challenge and orders them in descending order based on the average vote achieved. We are thus glad to proclaim the winner of the 2016 edition of the Rapid Mashup Challenge: *Smart-Composition* by Michael Krug, Fabian Wiedemann, Markus Ast and Martin Gaedke. Congratulations!

Of course, the ranking does not only communicate the winner of the Challenge but also some relative positioning of all the presented approached. Before going to fast interpretations or comparisons with the ranking of last year, we would however like to point out again what we already explained earlier in this volume: this year we accepted proposals of very different maturity (see the respective column in the table), in order to provide an as rich as possible picture of the ongoing activities of the community. But attention, the maturity of a presented approach significantly impacts also the other criteria of the evaluation, as an approach or tool that is not yet at the level of development the authors envision themselves, of course, cannot be expected to score high in those criteria

Table 1. Final ranking of the 2015 RMC based on the feedback gathered from the audience during the challenge (the smallest vote possible was 0 stars, the highest 5 stars)

Rank	Tool	Expressive power	Flexibility	Maturity	Intuitiveness	Demo effectiveness	Average
1	SmartComposition	3.73	3.77	3.55	3.45	3.68	3.64
2	FlexMash 2.0	3.42	3.15	3.77	3.42	3.35	3.42
3	EFESTO	2.50	2.44	3.00	3.38	2.50	2.76
4	Search-based mashups	2.67	2.56	3.72	2.33	2.44	2.74
5	Uduvudu Editor	2.88	2.71	2.33	2.42	2.75	2.62
6	Linked widgets	2.32	2.46	2.82	1.93	2.18	2.34
7	CAMUS	1.85	1.60	1.95	1.60	1.90	1.78
8	Toolet	1.50	1.61	1.17	1.50	1.33	1.42

that are still under development. In some cases, the presented tool was even still at the level of a proof of concept prototype; this is, for instance, the case of CAMUS and Toolet, two approaches that were still in a very early stage of development but that we nevertheless felt deserved some space in the Challenge in order to allow the authors to explain their ideas and to obtain constructive feedback from the audience. Therefore, the ranking should be read as a comparison of screenshots of approaches or instruments taken at a given instant of time during their development, some already in a rather mature phase, others still in the conception phase.

This being said, it is interesting to note that the winner of the Challenge is not the approach that scored best in terms of maturity. Instead that audience particularly appreciated its flexibility and the effectiveness of the demo, next to the expressive power of the approach. The approach that was assessed as the most mature, instead, was FlexMash 2.0, where the "2.0" already hints at the evolution the tool has undergone over the last years. The hard work by the authors has payed off. Also search-based mashups presented by Eduard Daoud (not included in this volume for time restrictions) were considered very mature, in line with the nature of this industrial contribution to the Challenge.

Looking at all votes together, it seems that the presented approaches can be grouped into three clusters: proof-of-concept prototypes (ranks 7–8), advanced prototypes (ranks 3–6) and production-ready instruments (ranks 1–2). Search-based mashups are an exception, which is an instrument that is actually used in production in industrial contexts; while this is acknowledged by the audience with a high maturity score, the other criteria lower the position of the approach in the overall ranking.

Last year, the distribution of the votes was rather narrow. This year, we notice a significant difference between the votes of the different approaches. This is fully in line with the observation that last year the compared tools were very similar in terms of their maturity, while this year there is much more variety in the maturity.

5   Limitations

As with all rankings based on subjective feedback, the key issue is participation. And the ranking provided in Table 1 is no exception. On average, the audience during the Challenge consisted of approximately 20–25 people, most of which also participated in the voting process. More specifically, all votes reported in the ranking are based on individual feedbacks collected from 8–14 participants. The authors participating in the Challenge were asked not to participate in the voting process for their own presentation; no issue regarding this rule was reported, and we trust in the correct, ethical conduct of all participants.

As for the comparison of mashup approaches themselves, our comment of last year is still valid: Given the wide variety of approaches to mashup tool design, both from research and industry, and the lack of standard or commonly accepted benchmarks to assess development tools, it remains difficult to give a fair comparison of mashup development approaches/tools. But we do not only re-confirm this statement and even must add that this year the comparison was even harder, given the different levels of maturity of the presented works.

During the challenge, tools were demonstrated by their own authors, something that may invalidate any claim of usability or accessibility, especially by end-user programmers, usually associated with mashup tools. However, since every tool was used by the corresponding authors, the fairness of the comparison is not affected. In the future, it could be an interesting option to allow also the audience to try the proposed instruments, at least in very simple design scenarios. This would allow the audience to obtain a better feeling especially of the intuitiveness criterion, but also of the maturity criterion.

6   Conclusion

Summing up, we consider this second edition of the Rapid Mashup Challenge a success, similar to the one of the first edition. The quality of both the presented works and the presenters was high, and the topics brought forward by the presenters as well as by the audience were stimulating. Compared to the first edition, which was characterized by a set of mashup approaches at a comparable level of maturity, this year the approaches selected for presentation span all phases of the development life cycle, from early prototypes to production-ready tools. While this on the one hand hindered to some extent the comparison of the approaches, on the other hand it however conveys a very positive message: research on mashups and Web-based composition technologies is a topic of continuing interest and strategic value to both industry and academia. Although mashups, that is, the integration of all kinds of Web resources, have percolated into common software engineering practice, there is a continuous need for cutting-edge research that investigates that potential, opportunities and pitfalls of new technologies as they emerge and that aims to conceptualize and abstract the respective underlying principles to facilitate their use.

The approaches presented in the context of the RMC do exactly this, some of which even with the goal of enabling non-programmers to take part in the development of composition-based applications. This volume represents tangible evidence of this effort and of the need to invest even further efforts into the directions outlined throughout this volume – directions we hope will be explored in the future editions of the Challenge.

After this second edition of the Challenge, we see that the challenge for the future of the Challenge is understanding how to reliably compare approaches that are as diverse as the ones that characterize the domain of assisted mashup development in an environment that is constantly changing and evolving. While in the first edition this was less evident, this year the problem emerged prominently. One key ingredient toward a more objective benchmarking of assistive mashup development techniques seems to be, as identified this year, a clear differentiation of the maturity levels of the competing approaches. Being the RMC a challenge that aims to provide a final ranking of approaches, also this year we proposed a possible (subjective) ranking; yet, as we pointed out, it is important to acknowledge that inside this ranking not all approaches are actually comparable. How to enable a fair comparison, if possible at all, is a question we leave to the Challenges to come.

Acknowledgment. We would like to thank all participants for their enthusiasm and the audience for their active help with the evaluation of the presented approaches. We would also like to thank Vasileios Triglianos for his help and support with the ASQ tool used to organize the voting process.

Reference

1. Triglianos, V., Pautasso, C.: Interactive scalable lectures with ASQ. In: Casteleyn, S., Rossi, G., Winckler, M. (eds.) ICWE 2014. LNCS, vol. 8541, pp. 515–518. Springer, Heidelberg (2014). doi:10.1007/978-3-319-08245-5_40

Author Index

Printed in the United States
By Bookmasters